UFO SIGHTINGS
in CANADA

True Stories, Strange Encounters and Cover-ups

Lisa Wojna

FOLK LORE PUBLISHING

The Publisher: Folklore Publishing
Website: www.folklorepublishing.com

Library and Archives Canada Cataloguing in Publication

Wojna, Lisa, 1962–

   UFO sightings in Canada: True stories, strange encounters and
cover-ups / Lisa Wojna.

Includes bibliographical references.

ISBN 978-1-926677-74-3

   1. Unidentified flying objects—Sightings and encounters—Canada. I. Title.

TL789.6.C3W54 2011   001.9420971   C2011-904140-5

Project Director: Faye Boer
Project Editor: Wendy Pirk
Proofreader: Kathy van Denderen
Production: Lisa Morley
Cover Image: © 2010 Thinkstock; © Photos.com
Photos: Title Page: © 2011 Thinkstock; © Shutterstock; back cover:
© Hemera Technologies

Produced with the assistance of the Government
of Alberta, Alberta Multimedia Development
Fund

**Government
of Alberta** ■

We acknowledge the financial support
of the Government of Canada through
the Canada Book Fund (CBF) for our
publishing activities.

 Canadian   Patrimoine
Heritage   canadien

PC: 5

Contents

Dedication

To all the things in life that defy explanation, and the one thing in life that never needs one

Acknowledgements

The topic of UFOs is so vast and the literature supporting and refuting claims, proven or unproven, is so abundant that it is impossible to pen any kind of book on the topic without referring to the huge body of research already in existence. With that in mind, I owe a huge debt of gratitude to the journalists, broadcasters, researchers, scientists, ufologists and concerned citizens everywhere who shared a story or provided information on the cases in this book.

In particular, I'd like to thank Chris Rutkowski, a Manitoba-born astronomer recognized the world over for his detailed and unbiased research into the field of UFO studies. For almost two decades, Rutkowski and his colleague and fellow researcher Geoff Dittman collated the information they amassed on documented sightings throughout the country and then published "The Canadian UFO Survey," an invaluable, one-of-a-kind document.

I'd also like to acknowledge Library and Archives Canada for their extensive collection of letters, reports, maps, photographs and government documents they've acquired, scanned and placed online so Canadians everywhere can learn more about some of our country's strange sightings. The literally thousands of entries provided first-hand information, and previously sealed records helped me ensure the stories in this book are as complete and rounded as possible.

As always, I extend a huge amount of gratitude to my editor, Wendy Pirk. A good editor has the ability to point out what is missing in each story, and in my case, more often than I care to admit, reins in my all-too-frequent tendency toward wordiness. This book would be so much less without her keen eye and sharp pen, and I thank her from the bottom of my heart.

Thanks also to my long-time mentor, Faye Boer, and the staff of Folklore Publishing.

And of course, I thank my ever-patient family. Once again you put up with my long hours in front of the computer and my panic when the deadline for this project came...and went.

Introduction

I believe that these extra-terrestrial vehicles and their crews are visiting this planet from other planets. Most astronauts were reluctant to discuss UFOs...I did have occasion in 1951 to have two days of observation of many flights of them, of different sizes, flying in fighter formation, generally from east to west over Europe.

–Major Gordon Cooper (NASA astronaut) in an address to the United Nations

AN OBSESSION WITH THE IDEA that more than stars populate the heavens and that other, significantly advanced civilizations inhabit far-away galaxies is as old as our earliest civilization. Cave paintings depicting strange objects in the sky have been discovered, the walls of ancient Egyptian tombs often sport images of unidentifiable creatures, and stories of odd happenings have haunted humankind and, quite honestly, made us bipeds a little nervous since the dawn of human time. What if aliens exist? What if they indeed possess technology far beyond anything we can imagine? And what if they land on our planet and take over? Would they want to befriend us or enslave us? Imaginings of what a potential interaction between humans and extraterrestrial life could involve are endless.

Of course, we've made pretty good use of those imaginings, including, but not limited to, the inspiration fuelling our film and television industry.

There was *The Man from U.N.C.L.E, Mork and Mindy*, countless series of *Star Trek, The X-Files* and *Star Wars*, just to mention some of the sitcoms, dramas and epic movies that captivated generations and made light of the possibility of connecting with this potential other-worldly presence.

Because of the advances in technology and communication in the 20th and 21st centuries, stories about allegedly real but strange, unexplained happenings now have a wider audience. The general public heard about what happened in Roswell, New Mexico, in July 1947; about the clusters of orbs hovering in the horizon and initiating an official U.S. Air Force response in Washington, DC, in 1952; and about the alleged alien abduction of Betty and Barney Hill, a couple travelling along the highway near Groveton, New Hampshire, in 1961.

The facts, at least the perceived facts, and fiction soon joined forces, and just about anyone with access to a radio or newspaper and who had heard of these or other stories developed their own theories about the possibility of a higher power watching over us. For some, that belief in a higher power has evolved from an image of an all-powerful, all-loving god to an idea of a superior civilization whose motives we cannot determine. Are we just puppets in a roadside show? Are we nothing more than experiments to be poked at and prodded, as some bizarre accounts of abductions have suggested? Are we dispensable and at the mercy of an alien race that could dispose of us on a whim?

Some authorities on the subject suggest that as much as 50 percent of the general population on this continent believe in the existence of UFOs. In 1996, according to an Angus Reid poll, 70 percent of Canadians believed that intelligent life exists somewhere else in the universe, and just over half of the people sampled believed extraterrestrials have already visited our planet. Even if, as some sources suggest, Canadians are a little less inclined to embrace the idea of alien civilizations than our neighbours to the south, a significant number of us—though we might not come out and say that we believe little green men exist—can't imagine that the life inhabiting this planet is the only life of its kind in the universe.

I can't say I've ever seen anything that could be called a UFO. But I have family members who claim to have witnessed a strange sight in August 1990 while camping in the Whiteshell Provincial Park in the middle of a stifling hot Manitoba summer.

The story involves my then-eight-year-old son Peter, his cousins, my sister and my brother-in-law. My parents and sister own two lakefront cabins on White Lake, and that summer Peter was spending some time visiting his cousins. One day the youngsters pitched a couple of tents in the front yard and camp outside for the night. It's always a thrill for the kids in the family to do this—feels a little dangerous even, especially with the amount of wildlife that likes to wander about in the dead of night.

As the kids were getting settled in their sleeping bags, they noticed a string of red, green and blue lights flickering. Because it was such a humid night, the adults on the scene reasoned that what they saw could have been the result of light being refracted against the moisture in the sky. But as they watched the strange phenomenon over the course of about four hours, the explanation seemed less and less likely.

On closer inspection, it looked as though the strange lights were lining the outer lip of some kind of unrecognizable airborne object. One moment the "aircraft" was stationary, as if it was somehow being suspended in mid-air. Then without warning it would jut up and down, or side to side, only to rush away in a violent frenzy and return just as quickly.

Of course the kids were convinced they'd seen a UFO. A little unnerved by the experience, they took shelter in the cabin and challenged the adults for an explanation. My level-headed, Type A sister remembers everyone standing in front of the picture window that night. She would never admit that she saw a UFO, but to this day she says she can offer no explanation for what they witnessed.

The following day, I arrived at the lake to visit the family and check on how my son was doing. The big news of the day was the UFO they'd seen the night before. I laughed, thinking how crazy they all were and what imaginations they had.

Then I did what I do whenever I'm at the lake—I took a walk to the resort to treat the youngsters to some ice cream. That's when I came face to face with something that could quite conceivably give their story some legitimacy.

There on the counter was a copy of the morning issue of the *Winnipeg Sun*, with its entire front page sporting a photograph of crop circles discovered near the small community of St. Francis Xavier. Now as it happened, we lived just about 20 kilometres west of St. Francis Xavier at the time, which was due west of the lake in the direction where Peter and his cousins say they spotted the strange object.

The two strange occurrences happening at roughly the same time, and both in such close proximity to where we and other members of our family lived, produced gooseflesh on my arms. Could it be possible that there was indeed something to the kids' story? Had we been surveyed by some other civilization hovering overhead?

According to reports filed by Chris Rutkowski to MUFON, (the Mutual UFO Network), the 59-foot-diameter (18 metre) crop circle near St. Francis Xavier was one of several crop circles that popped up around Manitoba that summer. A 62-foot-diameter (19 metre) circle was discovered on August 29 near Niverville, and several other, smaller circles were reported throughout the province—it was beginning to look like Manitoba farms were a big draw for extraterrestrial stopovers.

The vast majority of the time, a UFO sighting is only referred to as such for a short while because a little digging produces a rational explanation. But there are times when, after extensive investigation, a sighting remains unexplained, and that blip in the air remains unidentified. Either way, these incidents have tanta-lized residents in communities across this nation, provided fodder for coffee room chatter and contributed "evidence" for folks on either side of the debate.

Regardless of what your take on this issue was when you first cracked open the pages of this book, the stories that follow will likely challenge you to think outside of your personal box, just a bit. And at the end of the day, when you turn the last page in that final chapter, these tales may have answered a few of your questions—and left you with many others.

Part One

UFOs: THE BIG PICTURE

CHAPTER ONE

UFO Overview

Of course the flying saucers are real, and they are interplanetary.

> –Air Chief Marshall Lord Dowding,
> Royal Air Force, World War II,
> as quoted by Reuters in August 1954

In the Beginning

SIGHTINGS OF WHAT WERE CATEGORIZED as unidentified flying objects have dated back to prehistoric times. One of the more recent archaeological discoveries included a series of prehistoric cave paintings located about 70 kilometres from Raisen in India's state of Madhya Pradesh. According to an article published in the *Rajasthan Times* on February 17, 2010, the cave in question is located in a "dense jungle," and the paintings depict "a clear image of what might be an alien or ET in a space suit…along with a classical flying saucer shaped UFO." Wassim Khan, an archaeologist on the search expedition, went on record saying the paintings "might suggest beings from other planets have been interacting with humans since prehistoric times" and that these otherworldly beings might have helped establish human habitation on this planet we call Earth.

Of course claims like this aren't accepted today without a whole lot of speculation, scrutiny and outright skepticism. But back in the 1960s, theories about UFOs leaned more in favour of the possibility that there was life on other planets, or at the very least, officials were reluctant to rule it out altogether. Announcements of UFO sightings sent shivers down the spines of a public far more willing to explore the possibility that we are not alone in this universe. This was especially true following World War II, when the topic rose in media popularity and books and films pummelled a curious public with what, to a large extent, amounted to little more than unsubstantiated propaganda.

At the same time, reported sightings were linked to well-known and respectable figures such as businessman Kenneth Arnold. While flying past Washington's Mount Rainier in 1947, the hobby pilot said he'd seen "a group of nine high-speed...crescent-shaped objects" flying at speeds he'd estimated to be "several thousand miles per hour," making them look "like saucers skipping on water." Arnold was such an esteemed public figure in his day that his sighting prompted widespread media coverage, and the fact that he went public with what he saw encouraged others with similar experiences to do the same.

Spurred on by Arnold's story, along with an increase in reported sightings elsewhere in the United

States, Lieutenant General Nathan F. Twining of the U.S. Army initiated Project Sign. After reviewing countless reports of UFO sightings, Twining believed there was enough merit in the subject to consider conducting an investigation. While no one official was willing to jump up and down and claim extraterrestrial life existed and was attempting to communicate with inhabitants of our planet, the powers that be were concerned that someone was invading American air space. Perhaps it was the Russians or some other government regime with advanced aerospace technology, one theory suggested—it was a popular theory used to explain several sightings. Either way, the reports needed to be investigated.

Project Sign was disbanded in 1948 after only a year in operation: no firm conclusion as to the existence of extraterrestrial life was ever developed in the endeavour. But when one project closed its files, another often emerged. And while the investigative efforts of our neighbours to the south were considerably more active than those taking place in Canada, the authorities in our country were not silent on the issue. The country's Department of National Defence, in cooperation with several other governmental agencies, conducted a number of different studies into the matter, including Project Magnet from 1950 to 1954, and Project Second Story from 1952 to 1954. Additional, smaller-scale investigations revolved around notable reports the authorities believed warranted further attention.

What's in a Name?

It was United States Air Force captain Edward J. Ruppelt who first coined the phrase "unidentified flying object," or UFO, back in 1952 when he was heading up Project Blue Book, an investigation into what at the time seemed like an overwhelming accumulation of reported sightings from the public as well as a handful of reputable, well-known people.

The term "flying saucers" came about in part thanks to businessman Kenneth Arnold, who used the term to describe what he spotted during a flight over Mount Rainier in 1947. Ruppelt believed calling these unexplained sightings "flying saucers" or "flying disks," as was common at the time, misrepresented the phenomena. Ruppelt's view was that because there was usually no proof as to the origin of these appearances when they were first reported, and all anyone could say for certain was that they saw something hovering in the sky, any term used to refer to the phenomena should reflect that. Hence Ruppelt coined the phrase "unidentified flying object," which could point to anything from atmospheric phenomena or unauthorized foreign aircraft to spacecraft from another civilization.

Of course, neither Ruppelt nor any of his colleagues would ever admit to the American public that something like little green men from another planet actually existed—at least they wouldn't go on record saying such a thing. But it didn't matter what officials said. The public had developed its own thoughts on the matter, and in the minds of some there was good reason for concern.

In 1938, noted author Orson Welles whipped into a frenzy anyone who had a radio and was tuned in to the dramatization of *The War of the Worlds*; people thought what they were listening to was an actual news broadcast and that an extraterrestrial presence was taking over the world. In fact, some folks continued to believe that aliens were threatening to take over the world no matter how much effort went into trying to convince them otherwise.

In July 1947, just two months after Arnold's flying saucer experience, people throughout North America were thrust into another panic when Matt Brazell, a farmer living near Roswell, New Mexico, stumbled across some debris near his farm. The find caused concern because around the same time several people in the area filed independent reports saying they'd seen something strange in the sky. It was because of those well-publicized stories that Brazell reported his discovery to the authorities.

Military personnel initially went on record as saying the recovered items resembled a "crashed disk" of unknown origin, but then changed their tune, retracting their earlier comments and saying the crashed object was really a downed weather balloon. But by then it was too late to calm the nerves of an increasingly worried public. As with *The War of the Worlds* scenario, a disbelieving public was crying out that a cover-up was going on. There was no doubt in their minds; we earthlings were not alone in the universe.

First in North America

An Associated Press article from October 2007 pointed out that a poll conducted between the news agency and Ipsos, a global market research company, found one-third of the American population believed in the existence of UFOs. Even more startling was the discovery that 14 percent of the population said they'd actually seen one. Here in Canada, a 1997 survey conducted by the UFOlogy Research of Manitoba suggested as many as 9.6 percent of the Canadian public—which was about three million people at that time—believed they'd actually seen a UFO.

Needless to say, interest from such a large demographic of the North American public mandates some kind of formal research into the topic. Folks following the study of unidentified flying objects— also known as ufology—have dug through history books and sacred texts to find support for their theory that strange objects that suddenly appeared and then as quickly disappeared in the sky might just point to a civilization from another planet.

Some say the first UFO sighting officially recognized in North America took place in the Massachusetts Bay Colony in 1638. John Winthrop, an English Puritan and the first elected governor of the colony, recorded in his personal journal an event several of his colleagues witnessed:

...In this year one James Everell, a sober, discreet man, and two others, saw a great light in the night at Muddy River. When it stood still, it flamed up, and was about three yards square; when it ran, it was contracted into the figure of a swine: it ran as swift as an arrow towards Charlton, and so up and down about two or three hours...Diverse other credible persons saw the same light, after, about the same place...

Being a man of Christian conviction and a respected authority in the community, Winthrop considered every imaginable natural possibility for the cause of this sighting. That Everell could have witnessed a meteor bursting through the atmosphere was unlikely because his sighting took place over such a prolonged period of time.

Winthrop also considered the possibility that it was a gas of some kind, but he rejected the idea, largely based on the fact that Everell was such a credible witness. "This account of an ignis fatuus [a phosphorescent light that hovers over swampy grounds, also called "Swamp Gas," "will-o'-the-wisp," or "ghost lights"] may easily be believed on testimony less respectable than that which was adduced."

Unable to come to an adequate conclusion on the matter, Winthrop still denounced the sighting, saying that, "...some operation of the devil, or other power beyond the customary agents of nature, was probably imagined by relaters and hearers of that age..."

Winthrop couldn't find an explanation, but he didn't believe in the sighting anyway.

First in Canada

There are several suggestions about who actually recorded Canada's first UFO sighting, as well as where and when it took place. A group called ParaResearchers of Ontario states that Elizabeth Posthuma Simcoe, wife of John Graves Simcoe, who served as lieutenant-governor of the Province of Upper Canada (Ontario) from 1792 to 1796, is often touted as the first Canadian of European decent to record such a sighting in this country. The group quotes the following excerpt from her personal journals dated December 24, 1791:

> ...Dr. T. M. Nooth says a great light was observed last night in the air in a direction N.E. beyond St. Paul's Bay, which is 30 leagues below Québec, opposite Isle aux Coudres, in the St. Lawrence. He supposed an eruption had taken place from a volcano, which is believed from the reports of the Indians to be in those parts, and a fresh eruption might have taken place there, occasioned by an earthquake which was severely felt a few days since near St. Paul's Bay. However, there is much...conjecture in the supposition about the existence of this volcano...

A reference to several strange sightings in the area that month also appeared in the *Québec Gazette* in the form of letters to the editor from eyewitnesses. Some of these accounts pointed to the possibility of an earthquake or explosion that resulted in "a globe of fire appearing to the eye of the size of a 40-pound cannon ball," which was then seen "bursting with an explosion" in the sky above St. Paul's Bay.

Canadians today don't worry about earthquakes and volcanic eruptions, but these geological occurrences were occasionally reported around St. Paul's Bay and Québec's northern mountain area between the 17th and 19th centuries.

In his book *The Chronicles of the St. Lawrence*, Sir James MacPherson Le Moine refers to the "great earthquake of 1663" and two other earth shakers of significant impact, one in 1791—the very earthquake referred to in the letters sent to the *Québec Gazette* as well as in Elizabeth Posthuma Simcoe's journal entry—and another in 1870. Still, significant oddities in the stories that people shared led to the question of whether the sightings were actually a result of an earth-shaking disturbance, or if something else was responsible—something that defied explanation.

Another theory is that Jesuit missionaries might have recorded Canada's first UFO. According to a Canwest news article from August 8, 2006, the 17th-century sighting recorded in New France went something like this:

We saw fiery serpents [flying] *through mid-air, borne on wings of flame. Over Québec we beheld a great ball of fire, which illumined the night almost with the splendour of day, had not our pleasure in beholding it been mingled with fear, caused by its emissions of sparks in all directions.*

In his Hudson Bay journals, trailblazer David Thompson wrote about yet another early UFO sighting, which occurred in 1792 when he and another explorer were camping near a lake in northern Manitoba.

> *It was a meteor of globular form, it seemed to come directly at us, lowering as it came, when within 300 yards* [274 metres] *from me, it struck the River* [about 540 kilometres north of Winnipeg] *ice, with a sound like a mass of jelly, was dashed in innumerable luminous pieces and instantly expired...curiosity chained me to the spot.*

Thompson and his companion, Andrew, reasoned that perhaps what they'd seen was a meteor crashing, but the idea didn't make sense to Thompson. The "object" didn't behave like a meteor—it didn't have a tail and it made a noise. The next day, when Thompson and Andrew went to check for any evidence at the crash site, they could find none.

Two nights later, Thompson saw another potential meteor. He wrote, "...as it struck the trees, pieces flew from it and went out; as it passed by me striking the trees with the sound of a mass of jelly, I noticed [the meteorites]...."

Thompson set out to examine the crash site the day after that sighting. Again, the explorer found no evidence of the previous night's activities. None of it made any sense; Thompson knew what he'd seen and heard.

Project Y

In 1952, John Frost, chief design engineer responsible for special projects conducted by the A.V. Roe company, was part of a two-man team developing the technical criteria for an aircraft designed to resemble, and behave, like a UFO—or at least what the world at the time perceived UFOs to look and behave like. Initially, the body of the aircraft was to simulate a horseshoe or a spade. But there were problems with the first design, which was labelled as Project Y, and it was discarded.

But the idea wasn't completely tossed away. Frost continued to mull over plans to build a "radical aircraft design" consisting of a "circular planform, flat-riser aircraft," and he started working on Project Y2, also known as Project Silver Bug. One unique quality of the revamped design was that it had circular wings. It also must have addressed other, earlier concerns because it was scheduled for production in Avro's Malton, Ontario, plant.

By this point, Canada's federal government got on board with the project in a small and quiet way. The Defense Research Board (DRB) at that time had started taking an active interest in the possible existence of flying saucers and alien life forms through other projects. And there was talk that the Soviet Union had already developed a similar craft. This added a sense of urgency to Avro's proposal in the eyes of both the Canadian and American governments. Canada's DRB allegedly provided $300,000 to help fund the development of the project. But even with this help and interest from other military organizations such as the United States Air Force, the envisioned saucer never made it off the page and onto the runway.

Research Findings

Special interest groups largely conduct the study of UFOs in Canada. In fact, this is quite likely true of most countries. While the occasional academic panel or governmental agency makes a quick foray into the arena of UFO research from time to time, their presence in the field is often little more than a response to public or military concerns.

The small Newfoundland community of Harbour Mille is a great example of what a public furor can do as far as attracting an official presence in an investigation is concerned. A sighting in January 2010, which was observed by many unrelated people who all told similar stories about their experience, was so compelling that even the Canadian military eventually got involved. Witnesses weren't suggesting that aliens had landed; they were concerned some military activity might be going on, and if that was the case, they wanted an official response to the situation. Was it possible Canada's east coast was being monitored by a foreign government? Was someone conducting unauthorized experiments in the ocean?

Whatever the residents of Harbour Mille saw, their public outcry was so powerful that the sighting warranted national media coverage. "It appeared to come out of the ocean...it was like it was in the middle of the bay," Emmy Pardy told CBC News. "It's kind of scary because you don't know if something is being set off out in the bay, [or] if someone is doing experiments."

Was it possible test missiles were being fired off the shores of the French islands of Saint-Pierre and Miquelon? And for those with more sensational imaginations, could it be possible that Canada's Atlantic coastline was being visited by intelligent beings from another planet?

The story of Harbour Mille eventually petered out without officials coming to a satisfying conclusion about what residents claimed they'd seen that cool January day. Authorities did say Canada was never in any danger, but no one was willing to chime in with a clear explanation about what was actually going on.

Over the last several decades, one of the most vocal groups delving into the topic of UFOs in this country was the UFOlogy Research of Manitoba. For 20 years, members of this group, which included Winnipeg author, teacher, astronomer and UFO enthusiast Chris Rutkowski, conducted annual surveys on reports of sightings throughout the country.

The last survey, compiled by Rutkowski and Geoff Dittman and published in February 2009, reviewed 1004 sightings filed in Canada in 2008—an "all-time record high number of reports in one year," according to the final document. The survey catalogued everything: the number of witnesses, the descriptions of what witnesses saw, the duration that the object was visible and the location and time of day it appeared. According to the summary, "almost half of all UFO sightings were of simple lights in the sky" and often correlated with natural occurrences or civilian and military aircraft. Some accounts of strange phenomena included objects shaped like "triangles, spheres and boomerangs" or "disc-shaped objects," though reports of this nature were rare.

The survey examined reasons why an increase in the number of sightings are reported each year and suggested that Internet access, which adds to the ease of reporting, might be one consideration. The fact that the media often publishes some of the more sensational stories, as well as the perception that people who report strange events are less stigmatized than in the past, might work together to encourage more people to go to the authorities with their stories. Regardless, the increase in reports—from 141 in 1989 to the most recent 1004 in 2008—is staggering.

The survey is quick to point out that all but 10 percent of those 1004 reports were comfortably explained. Even though some sightings remained classified as being of unknown origin, only one percent was considered "high quality unknowns," meaning they were still unexplained after "above-average levels of investigation and documentation."

Although Rutkowski cautioned readers that, "there is still no incontrovertible evidence that some UFO cases involve extraterrestrial contact," he also encouraged further study into that one percent of sightings that begged for additional attention. "The continued reporting of UFOs by the public and the increase in numbers of UFO reports suggests a need for further examination of the phenomenon by social, medical and/or physical scientists," he stated. "This is a fascinating field for study, whether one believes or doubts that UFOs are 'real.'"

Because the UFOlogy Research of Manitoba (UFO-ROM) has been involved to a great extent in the studies of UFO sightings in this country, the majority of the statistics on UFOs have been gathered through their efforts. A review of the 20-year time span from which UFOROM collected information suggested the most popular location for reports of unidentified flying objects is a bit of a tug-of-war, year after year, between BC and Ontario, with BC edging out the larger province with a total of 2508 sightings versus 2294.

In 2007, Calgary placed first for the highest number of sightings in a city, while Toronto recorded the highest number of strange objects in the sky for a metropolitan area, with 79 reports filed with officials. July and August are Canada's hottest months in more ways than just the temperature: most sightings are recorded during those months. Ufologists suggest the increase in reports at that time of the year could be because more folks are outside, especially between 9:00 PM and midnight, when most sightings take place.

The UFOROM survey also stresses that the majority of sightings are nothing more than strange lights in the sky that are easily explained:

Less than two percent of all reported UFO cases in 2008 were close encounters...the current popular interest in abductions and sensational UFO encounters is based not on the vast majority of UFO cases but on the very tiny fraction of cases which fall into the category of close encounters. The endless speculation of what aliens may or may not be doing in our airspace seems almost completely unconnected to what are actually being reported as UFOs.

Over the years, a seemingly endless number of police reports and government documents have been collected and filed, despite the fact that not every person who experiences something this bizarre is comfortable turning to the more traditional authorities. Starting in 2007, the Government of Canada opened the various files collected by the military, RCMP and other officials on the subject. An estimated 9500 documents, collected between 1947 and the 1980s, were released to Library and Archives Canada and are now open to the public for viewing. If you have the Internet, you can check out all 9500 documents. Like the results from UFOROM's decades' worth of surveys, many of the reports in the archives were resolved with a simple, logical explanation. Several, however, remain unresolved, and while some of the officials filing the reports on these cases have offered what they thought were reasonable explanations, a clear answer hasn't been forthcoming.

At the time of this writing, more than two years have passed since UFOROM published its 2008 survey. Sadly, members of the group found it necessary to pull back some of its research efforts, and the organization has not published a survey for 2009 or 2010. Rutkowski and Dittman explain it this way:

It should be reported that the preparation of this Survey is becoming quite challenging. Few UFO investigators or researchers actually submit case data to UFOROM anymore, requiring considerable searching of online sources. And, although many sites post information about UFO sightings, very little actual UFO investigation is being conducted. In fact, it could be said that the science of UFO investigation has nearly become extinct. This does not bode well for an area of study that is under constant criticism by debunkers wishing to prove the unscientific nature of the subject.

There are other small interest groups and individual efforts that have voiced opinions on the issue of UFOs in Canada from time to time. In 2002, Brian Vike, formerly of Houston, BC, established the HBCCUFO Research organization and website. In 2009, Vike, who had developed a solid reputation of professionalism, dedication and concern for both the topic of UFOs and the people who reported seeing them, pulled back from the field of study for a while, citing health concerns as a motivator for his actions. Others took over the website he established and continue to monitor sightings from around the world. But recent posts suggest Vike's love for mystery and researching the unknown has pulled him back into the fold; he now writes a blog entitled "The Vike Factor: Into the Paranormal," and Vike continues to collect stories of sightings from the world over.

Jim Moroney, executive director for the Alberta Municipal Health and Safety Association and part-time college and university instructor, is another Canadian source on the topic of UFOs. Moroney has more than 25 years of experience in the field and has used his skills as a public speaker, along with his formal education in "science, transpersonal psychology and health and safety," to help others understand the complexities surrounding the issue.

Unexplained objects and strange lights in the sky have been around since time immemorial. They will continue to stir the imaginings of Earth's inhabitants until the end of time, or until a concrete understanding of the UFO phenomenon is finally achieved. In the meantime, investigation into past and current sightings is ongoing.

CHAPTER TWO

Canadian UFO Station
a World First

...the existence of a different technology is borne out by the investigations which are being carried on at the present time in relation to flying saucers.... I feel that the correlation between our basic theory and the available information on saucers checks too closely to be mere coincidence.

–Wilbert B. Smith, Geo-Magnetics,
Department of Transport, November 21, 1950

Project Magnet

IT DIDN'T START OUT AS A QUEST to prove or explain the existence of UFOs—at least, that wasn't the official reason provided to the media for the establishment of a laboratory working on a classified project for the Department of Transportation (DOT) back in 1950.

Since shortly after his graduation from the University of British Columbia, with a degree in electrical engineering, Wilbert B. Smith had been devoting a considerable amount of his time researching the earth's magnetosphere. Smith, who was a senior radio engineer with the DOT in 1950, had theorized that it might be possible to manipulate the earth's magnetic field and use it as an energy source to propel vehicles. Operating on this theory, and with the backing of several government officials, he formed Project Magnet.

By the time he penned his first report on the subject, in November 1951, it looked like Smith might have been on to something. His summary explained how he and his researchers had managed to extract enough of the earth's magnetosphere to "operate a voltmeter at approximately 50 milliwats." A voltmeter is a calibrated instrument used for measuring electrical potential. "This tells you how much energy a charged particle will gain if it moves a certain distance, so if there is a huge potential (lots of volts) then the energy gain is high," explained Christopher Wiebe, associate professor at the University of Winnipeg.

Smith and his team used their findings to measure the earth's magnetic flow, and from the information they collected, they believed the results were promising. In Smith's own words, researchers were on the "track of something that may prove to be the introduction to a new technology."

But Smith's interest in this theory was fuelled by more than just a desire to discover a new technology. He had read an article on flying saucers a few years before approaching Dr. Omond McKillop Solandt, with a daring idea he wanted to with incorporate into the research being conducted with Project Magnet. Solandt at the time was founding chairman of the Canadian Defence Research Board (DRB).

Like a large segment of the population in the '50s, Smith was intrigued by an increase in the number of reports by people who said they'd witnessed an unidentified flying object—reports filed with reputable agencies, including the United States Air Force, the Royal Canadian Air Force (RCAF) and what at the time was known as Canada's Department of Transport (now Transport Canada).

As a man of science, Smith was well aware of the possible explanations that could account for many of these sightings. He also believed that any time a new science was discovered, it was because people stepped outside of the box and pushed beyond current understanding. Any scientist worth merit couldn't ignore the question "What if?" and would do everything possible to study a problem; as far as Smith was concerned, the sharp increase in reliable and credible UFO sightings seemed to indicate there was a mystery worth delving into.

Could aliens from another planet who were built like us but had acquired far superior technology to anything humankind had been able to master actually exist? After all, the universe was infinitely wide and deep, and science's limited knowledge could not adequately argue against the possibilities of life on other planets—especially when we could only identify a handful of planets from Earth's vantage point.

What if, Smith reasoned, extraterrestrial visitors not only existed but also hovered overhead a lot more frequently than even the most ardent ufologist might suggest? And what if they actually powered their spacecraft by doing what he'd suggested might be possible—extracting energy from the earth's magnetic field?

Smith's arguments sounded plausible enough to Solandt, who eventually backed the engineer's plans, even though some years later he would deny that connection. Smith's plans also won the approval of Commander C.P. Edwards, who served as the Deputy Minister of Transport for Air Services.

By December 1950, Project Magnet received the official approval it needed to get the ball rolling, both in regards to its study of the earth's magnetic field and the possibility of extraterrestrial traffic visiting our planet's atmosphere.

Although Smith had publicly linked his study of geomagnetism and research to the UFO phenomenon, the otherworldly connection was downplayed. According to Smith's 1952 report on Project Magnet, various arms of the federal government were on board with the idea that a "detailed study of the saucer phenomenon" was essential, as long as it was made "within the framework of existing establishments." In other words, officials agreed that the study of UFOs was warranted, but they didn't want to spend too much money on the project.

A Second Project

Still, some government funding must have been funnelled directly to the study of UFOs because Project Second Story, also sponsored by the DRB, was formed the same year as Smith's report. The purpose of Project Second Story was "solely dedicated to dealing with 'flying saucer' reports."

Solandt chaired the group's inaugural meeting on April 22, 1952. Attended by several representatives from the DRB, the meeting's first order of business was to determine if an independent, serious and organized effort into the investigation of UFO sightings was necessary and if so, the scope of investigation members of the group would undertake.

Research conducted by the U.S. Air Force was also discussed, along with the fact that their project had been discontinued because of "nil returns" for their efforts. But it was also recognized that government investigations into the topic had recently re-opened but were now "classified."

When it came to Canadian sightings, government officials determined that "precise and realistic details were lacking" in reports collected, so before establishing a committee to interrogate witnesses and log information they first had to develop a format to follow.

Members of Project Second Story were responsible for collecting detailed information based on a questionnaire specially designed to "minimize the personal equation." Simply speaking, interrogating witnesses was the first step in an investigation that relied a great deal on "deductive reasoning," and the questionnaire was designed to be as objective as possible.

Committee members then assessed these reports by using a mathematical formula that helped determine the reliability of the sightings. The formula helped researches acquire a number that would, in turn, allow them assign a "weighting factor" to each event. According to Smith:

> Sightings may be grouped according to certain salient features, and the combined weight of all pertinent observations with respect to these features may be determined by applying Peter's formula, which is a standard mathematical technique for determining probable error...where ro is the probable error of the mean, n is the number of observations and v is the probable error of each observation, that is, unity minus the weighting factor.

Once a report had been assigned a weighting factor, the next step in the analysis of a sighting was to sort the observation into the "compartment" it best fit into based on the pattern of that particular sighting. Smith explained that sightings could be placed into one of two categories: "those about which we know something and those about which we know very little."

Smith then evaluated the 25 sightings reported through the project in 1952. He applied his formula to obtain a weighting factor, sorted the sightings into categories, and then decided which of the several unexplained events pointed to the possibility that extraterrestrial beings visited our planet. Smith divided the 25 sightings into one of 11 groups. Seven of the sightings were likely "normal objects" such as meteors, aircraft, balloons and the like. Four sightings were likely "material, strange objects" and another three were listed as "immaterial, electrical phenomena."

The remaining 11 sightings were filed under the category of "strange objects." Smith further went on record stating, "the probability definitely favours the alien vehicle class, with the secret missile included with a much lower probability."

In Smith's mind there was very little doubt that an alien presence was visiting our planet in vehicles that had technology far surpassing anything humans had developed at that time, or since.

From a study of the sighting reports… it can be deduced that the vehicles have the following significant characteristics. They are a hundred feet [30 metres] or more in diameter; they can travel at speeds of several thousand miles per hour; they can reach altitudes well above those which would support conventional aircraft or balloons; and ample power and force seem to be available for all required manoeuvres. Taking these factors into account, it is difficult to reconcile this performance with the capabilities of our technology, and unless the technology of some terrestrial nation is much more advanced than is generally known, we are forced to the conclusion that the vehicles are probably extraterrestrial in spite of our prejudices to the contrary.

Anticipating the argument that the sightings were the result of an "optical phenomenon," Smith was equipped with a scientific reason as to why that explanation couldn't be the case. He explained that researchers made every effort to identify each unexplained sighting through known atmospheric occurrences and none of those explanations fit because of "...the geometrical laws dealing with optics generally and which we have never yet found cause to doubt, plus the wide discrepancies in the order of magnitude of the light values which must be involved in any sightings so far studied. Furthermore, introducing an optical system might explain an image in terms of an object, but the object still requires explaining."

Smith didn't waver from his stance that many unexplained reports were authentic sightings that didn't qualify as optical phenomena. He reiterated his argument years later in an interview with Canadian Press reporter Gerald Waring:

My own opinion is that the reports are valid. The optical illusion explanation is lovely, but in every sighting there is always some factor which rules it out. So we've decided to learn just what flying saucers are.

The Research Continues

Any object flying overhead would in all likelihood produce measurable, physical effects. Sound waves, fluctuations in airflow, possibly even gravity waves, if they could be proven to exist—these were only some of measurements researchers could have captured if

Project Magnet had been supplied with the necessary equipment.

It wasn't long before just such an appropriately equipped research station became a reality.

In 1952, the Defence Research Chemical Laboratory (DRCL) and the Defence Research Electronics Laboratory (DREL) came together to establish a new research campus. It was at this facility at Shirley's Bay, located on the Ottawa River just west of Canada's capital city, that Smith and his team established a "hut" fully equipped with "a compass type magnetometer, a gamma ray counter, a radio set and gravimeter."

A gravimeter "is designed to detect and record gamma rays, magnetic fluctuations, radio noises and gravity and mass changes in the atmosphere." Each of the four instruments was responsible for manipulating one of four pens connected to a recorder, and whenever they collected any data, that information was then transferred to a paper reading.

The Shirley's Bay hut soon earned the reputation as being the world's first UFO station. Researchers were hoping that in time the facility would provide them with some measurable data they could study. At the very least, they were hoping to obtain qualitative information that could help determine if gravity waves actually existed, and if so, how to detect them, how to generate these waves and what they might be used for.

Between 1953 and 1962, the world was experiencing another, more concrete stressor. Two of its most powerful countries were going through major political changes. Dwight Eisenhower replaced Harry Truman as president in January 1953. And on the other side of the world, Nikita Khrushchev took over the leadership of the Soviet Communist Party following the death of Joseph Stalin. Proponents of communism clashed with the capitalists' worldview, and the leaders of both administrations struggled for superiority, fuelling fears of nuclear war and the subsequent annihilation of the human race. Depending on who you asked, the idea that little green men were floating overhead might have been preferable to thoughts that the Russians had developed some kind of high-tech war machine.

While researchers were hoping to collect data, and the public continued reporting strange objects in the sky, the RCAF was petitioning the federal government for funds to develop a "supersonic twin-engine, two-seat interceptor." In 1953, the A.V. Roe Company (later known as Avro Canada Ltd.) acquired a contract to develop the specialized aircraft.

It appeared that a race was running on two fronts: the race to acquire the world's most advanced war machine, and the race to discover if we really are alone in this universe.

Smith was about to earn Canada a reputation for logging the world's only proof that something was indeed invading our country's airspace. But what exactly that "something" was would remain a mystery.

"All Unusual Occurrences Are Investigated"

On April 11, 1953, the Royal Canadian Air Force instructed officials at all its stations to follow a detailed set of regulations when it came to collecting, assessing and sharing information about unidentified flying objects. In particular, internal correspondence from the RCAF stated that they were "most anxious... not to have any publicity given" to the subject of flying saucers or, as they preferred to refer to the phenomenon, unexplained sightings.

In answer to any inquiries by the press concerning the RCAF's assessment of any particular incident, or the existence of "flying saucers" generally, it should be stated that ALL unusual occurrences are investigated as a matter of routine, and that, as far as is known, no conclusions have been drawn from past investigations.

Someone must have forgotten to give Smith that memo.

Smith was quoted in several newspaper articles shortly after the opening of the Shirley's Bay observatory, unabashedly touting the saucer-spotting station and its mandate. And on August 8, 1954, after researchers spent months watching "the sensitive gravimeter in vain," it started behaving strangely. Although it had "skipped a beat" on occasion when a large jet passed overhead, the gravimeter's movements never continued for any length of time—until that day. "[At] 3:01 PM the gravimeter began acting strangely," Smith wrote of the event:

First it waved, drawing a thin, dark line on the graph paper being used to measure the movements of the instruments. Without further warning the gravimeter went wild. All evidence indicated that a real unidentified flying object had flown within feet of the station.

Neither Smith nor any of his researchers could provide an explanation for the gravimeter's unusual behaviour. The gravimeter tripped the alarms hooked up to the instrument panel, and researchers rushed outside hoping to catch a glimpse of whatever it was that had obviously invaded the local airspace.

Unfortunately, the area was engulfed in fog. Everything looked like pea soup. Smith would later explain that the "overcast was down to 1000 feet [305 metres], so whatever was up there, whatever it was that generated the sharp variation, was concealed behind clouds." It looked like whatever caused the gravimeter to move would remain a mystery.

Still, Smith was anxious to share the news.

The *Globe and Mail* published an article on the "blip" on August 10. Its headline declared that "Canadian Scientists [were] First!" and posited the question whether researchers had inadvertently detected "a flying saucer."

Smith went on record saying he was "convinced that the deflection on the gravimeter was not caused by an aircraft." He did caution reporters that researchers at the station were trying to determine if there had been some kind of glitch in the instrumentation. And he stressed that the recordings gathered from whatever had flown overhead couldn't prove that a flying saucer had passed by.

However, Smith also emphasized that it was the first time he and his team couldn't explain the instrument's behaviour, and he declared that they now had a mystery on their hands. "We must now ask ourselves what it could have been," he said.

Two days after the article appeared in the news paper, the Department of Transport decided its three years of research into the origin of unidentified flying objects hadn't produced enough data to "reach any definite conclusion, and since new data appear to be similar to data already studied, there seems to be little point in carrying the investigation any further on an official level." With that, DOT announced it would "discontinue any further study of Unidentified Flying Objects, and Project Magnet which was set up for this purpose, will be dropped."

Strange though it may seem, Smith was still named a contact for those who wanted to report any new information and sightings. The DOT was quick to add that Smith's involvement in any UFO studies was being conducted "on a purely unofficial basis."

Life After Shirley's Bay

Smith continued to work for the DOT for several years following his stint at Shirley's Bay. While he was cautious not to discuss his views on the existence of UFOs from an official perspective, he wasn't averse to sharing his personal opinion on the matter. "I am convinced there are flying saucers," he was once quoted as saying a couple of years following the demise of Project Magnet, "but I'm in the unhappy position of the police chief who knows who robbed the bank but can't prove it in court."

Several sources suggest Smith's view that UFOs indeed exist in some form remained an intrinsic part of the man's psyche until his untimely death from cancer in 1962. Some of Smith's writings allegedly point to the existence of alien life from several planets and contain his own privileged communication with "occupants of UFOs." He claimed that these aliens were just like us, only about 500 years advanced technologically and at a "variety of stages of evolvement."

In Smith's own words, he had "spent too many hours conversing with people from elsewhere to have any doubts about their reality or that they are what they claim to be," and that "those of us who have been fortunate enough to have made contact with these people have learned a great deal, and profited greatly through this knowledge, in those things which really count, which we can take with us."

As fantastic as some of Smith's views apparently were, he was also a brilliant thinker and a leader in his field. After his death, he was awarded the Lieutenant-Colonel Keith S. Rogers Memorial Engineering Award for dedicated service in the advancement of Technical Standards in Canadian Broadcasting.

The research hut at Shirley's Bay still exists. And it's only prudent that officials investigate when reports of an unexplained sighting are filed. But whether or not the extent of the research is warranted is up to interpretation.

Either way, Smith's findings remain a curious story in the annals of Canada's strange but true UFO tales.

Part Two

THE SIGHTINGS

CHAPTER THREE

British Columbia

We all move on the fringes of eternity and are sometimes granted vistas through fabric of illusion. Many refuse to admit it: I feel a mystery exists. There are certain times, when, as on the whisper of the wind, there comes a clear and quiet realization that there is indeed a presence in the world, a nonhuman entity that is not necessarily inhuman.

–Ansel Adams, photographer
and environmentalist

Prince George: A Hotbed of Mystery

THE ONLY WAY TO REALLY APPRECIATE the vast expanse of wilderness that makes up the majority of British Columbia's 944,735 square kilometres of land is to secure a window seat and fly across the length and breath of the province on a clear, sunny day. The kilometre after kilometre of white-capped mountain peaks, separated by little more than the occasional narrow valley or meandering river, is nothing short of breathtaking.

To see such a large expanse of untamed and unclaimed Crown land in North America is a rare treat.

Many areas are simply inaccessible, but the province also has numerous provincial, federal and regional parks; some spots are set aside as protected agricultural reserves and an additional 14 percent of its land base has been classified as "protected" by provincial and federal governments.

And although the province's population of roughly 4,511,000 catapults BC into third place when it comes to the most populated provinces in Canada, most of those residents are concentrated in the Lower Mainland and in the towns and villages that dot some of the few major highways.

Add all these factors together and there's a lot of natural wilderness along Canada's western front that is basically uninhabited by humans except, perhaps, by the occasional squatter. Such an expansive and untouched wilderness means big game animals, such as cougars, grizzlies, wolves and mountain goats, have a huge territory to inhabit.

BC's wilderness has also provided a perfect haven for draft dodgers fleeing the United States. It has offered disenfranchised groups such as the Spirit Wrestlers, also known as the Doukhobors, a place where they could settle and embrace the freedom to follow their unique beliefs and lifestyles. The province has sometimes also been the answer to lost souls looking for a simpler way of life. And it has offered some folks the chance to adopt an earthy, rugged lifestyle that is not as readily available in other parts of this vast country.

BC also could, in theory, be a perfect hiding place for all sorts of creatures that don't like to attract too much attention to themselves. You know, those shy beasts that are the basis of many of British Columbia's myths and legends.

Ogopogo, the 12- to 15-metre-long water monster said to be living in Okanagan Lake, has captured the imagination of area residents since its first documented sighting back in 1872. There's the sea serpent Caddy, a strange, long-necked creature with a horse-like head and flippers—more than 300 sightings over the last two centuries have suggested it still lives along the Pacific coast. Another tale speaks of the discovery of a strange animal in the stomach of a whale harvested off Haida Gwaii (the Queen Charlotte Islands) in 1937.

And then, of course, there's everybody's favourite—Big Foot. The beast apparently stands more than 2 metres high and rushes to hide as soon as it's spotted by a human, except in the case of prospector Albert Ostman, who insisted he'd been held captive by a group of these creatures for seven days. The stories of sightings of this ape-like creature are so prolific that Green Point Park, a 20-hectare park nestled along the east side of Harrison Lake, was renamed Sasquatch Park in 1968 in honour of the elusive giant.

Given these stories, it makes sense that UFOs, which some consider to be the most evasive and mysterious creatures of all, would make frequent visits to the remote regions of this magnificent province.

A New Year, A New Sighting?

The sun sets early in January, especially in the northern reaches of British Columbia. But the darkness of night in the dead of winter doesn't necessarily spell cold in a part of the country where inversions often result in mild temperatures.

It was the first of the month—the first day in a new year—and several residents of Prince George were out and about doing chores or replenishing their cupboards after the previous night's revelry. Sometime between 5:00 and 6:00 PM, Walter Webster was making his way along Fifth Avenue toward Alward and Burden streets when he noticed a strange glow in the sky. The insurance salesman was so startled by the sight that he pulled into the Fifth Avenue Shell Service Station and approached station attendant Donald Cook and the customer he was serving, Grant Magnuson.

Webster rushed up to the men and pointed to the glow, and for a time all three residents noted every detail and pondered what on earth they were seeing. They all agreed the object was floating along at an altitude of between 610 and 3050 metres and was about one-eighth the size of the moon. It was moving—they could see it move very slowly, but they couldn't hear it making any sound. And it was glowing a "yellow-ish orange" colour but appeared to dim and brighten alternately.

The three Prince George residents watched the object for some time before Webster decided to head home.

He was anxious to tell his wife, Arlene, about his sighting and was surprised when she said she'd seen the same object just before six o'clock that evening. Her description corresponded with that of her husband. She agreed the strange dot in the sky sometimes appeared very bright indeed, and then at other times it was quite faint. Unlike her husband, she didn't have a clear enough view from her vantage point to make out a shape—Walter thought a square object was attached to the bottom of the "glowing" sphere. He also noticed that the top of the sphere looked like it sported a design or had "diagonal straps" fastened across it.

Shortly before Walter was driving along Fifth Avenue, Geoff Richmond and his family were also travelling that same neighbourhood. Richmond guessed it was about 5:30 PM when he, his wife and three teenaged children noticed a strange, spherical object floating across the sky. The postal worker didn't stop his car, so his attention to detail wasn't as thorough as that of the other witnesses.

Still, Richmond guessed the dot in the sky was about 1/20th the size of the moon, which was a little smaller than what Walter had suggested, perhaps because of the location where Richmond had spotted the sphere or the fact that it was travelling away from him. Other than the size discrepancy, Richmond concurred with the description of the object given by other witnesses.

In the same general area of Prince George, sometime between 6:30 and 7:00 PM, Ernest Webster was outside his Radcliff Drive home with his binoculars, peering into the night sky. Ernest, of no relation to Walter, was an assistant manager with the Civic Properties Commission for the City of Prince George. He'd seen a strange glow suspended in the air along the horizon that had piqued his interest, and he was curious about what it might be. As a civil servant, he was also likely interested in identifying the object in case residents in the area phoned in with questions about it. Like other observers who'd ventured to make a report, Ernest described the object as a "radiant orange glow" that would brighten suddenly, and then fade away until he'd think it had vanished, only to see it reappear again.

As one resident after another witnessed the strange phenomenon over Prince George that January night, calls started flowing into the Prince George detachment of the RCMP. Usually a single, strange sighting wouldn't cause much more than a cursory response. Checking out the local radar to make sure no airplanes were in trouble was typically the first order of business. Quite often a report wasn't even filed.

Of course, there have been situations when strange objects in other parts of the country caused a fervour, especially if the sighting was unique or if several people witnessed the phenomenon. With so many reports coming in about the Prince George sighting, officers on duty recognized the need to unearth an answer to the mystery.

And the sooner the better.

One tip phoned in by a visitor from the Netherlands sounded promising in that it provided a clue about what people might have seen. Victor Imhoff and his wife noticed a flying object around 5:15 that same afternoon. The couple was travelling by taxi to the home on Johnson Street where they were staying. The taxi was also travelling along Fifth Avenue, near Watrous Street, when the couple first noticed what looked like an orange, spherical object about 3 or 4 feet (one metre) in diameter. At the time Imhoff guessed it was hovering fairly close to the ground, perhaps 200 feet (60 metres) in the air, so he got a pretty good view of it.

From Imhoff's description, officers reasoned that the enigma might just be some kind of balloon. With this in mind, investigators called Frank Kerbrat, the officer in charge at the Department of Transport, to see if anyone had released a weather balloon. Kerbrat confirmed that one had been released in the area on January 1. For a while, it seemed as though the mystery surrounding this sighting had been solved.

Or had it?

Over the course of the next few days, additional reports were called in to the RCMP. On January 3, William McLeod reported his version of a strange glowing object floating across the horizon. The next day another resident came forward with a similar New Year's Day experience. And on January 5, Martin Pearson telephoned in with his report. Each of these reports were documented and kept on file.

Although investigators were making inquiries into the sightings, a definitive answer appeared to be as elusive as ever. At least it looked that way until the wee hours of January 4. William Dow was looking out his window shortly after midnight that morning when he noticed something odd wafting down from the sky and into the backyard of his home on Burden Street. Curious, Dow pulled on a pair of boots, grabbed his coat and made his way to check out what the object was. The unimpressive-looking contraption appeared to be nothing more than a plastic laundry bag with "one end held open with circular construction of drinking straws. A cross, which was formed in the centre with the help of two straws, had a number of birthday candles attached to it with the use of straight pins. The top end of the bag was made secure by taping it with Scotch Tape."

According to the official file on the glowing object Walter Webster had first reported, Dow either did not know about the earlier reports of UFO sightings or he didn't associate his find with the other reports, at least not until January 9. That's when he finally approached the RCMP and told them about the downed "balloon" in his backyard. Dow's information sounded promising, and the RCMP wasted no time in visiting the man's home to examine the downed balloon. With Dow's permission, officers brought the apparently homespun object to the station to examine and photograph it. They determined the object was a homemade device that was powered through the air by the heat from the lighted candles secured in its base. Simply put, it was like a mini air balloon.

Officers concluded that the unidentified flying object was more than likely either a weather balloon or this makeshift craft. That conclusion was backed by the fact that most of the sightings took place in fairly close proximity to one another, which was also the area where the downed "balloon" was eventually located. Officials declared the entire scenario was likely the work of "ingenious children," although no one was ever identified.

The residents of Prince George could rest easy knowing they weren't being monitored by life forms from another planet, at least not this time. But a quick answer to unexplained sightings certainly doesn't happen all the time, and an unsolved event has a way of making people feel mighty uncomfortable— especially those folks who had the close encounter of an unexplained kind.

Smithers: Up Over Yonder Mountains

I turned off all lights inside and outside the house to make sure that what I saw [the previous night] *and am seeing again tonight is not a reflection...This moving, glowing object I'm seeing at least 5 miles away is fluctuating from what looks like to be treetop level to higher. I am certain that the red UFO is in fact there in the night sky and is moving around in a daring manner as if searching for something....*

–an anonymous report from Massey, Ontario, dated May 12, 2011, as published in the reports section of the UFO Casebook website

Hovering Lights

People who have visited, or have had the privilege to live in, Smithers, BC, like to call the community one of Canada's best-kept secrets. The small, alpine-themed village is nestled at the foot of Hudson Bay Mountain in northern British Columbia's Bulkley Valley, which is located along Highway 16 at the midway point between Prince George and Prince Rupert. It is home to about 6000 residents. Being such a northern and remote location, it's not uncommon to see an errant moose wandering down one of the town's streets or in someone's front yard with a calf or two. And if you're hiking along the trails of Riverside Park, located on the town's northern corner, you could conceivably happen along a mama bear with her cubs, or find yourself being followed by the neighbourhood fox and her kits. Somehow the stars seem so much closer to the ground in Smithers, and on a bright night the snow-capped mountains set off a luminous glow.

Shortly after 2:30 AM on February 20, 2003, a young mother living in the Railway Avenue area of Smithers had just finished feeding her new baby and was getting ready to return to bed when she noticed something outside. Her living room window directly faced the ski runs on Hudson Bay Mountain, and her blinds were open just enough so as not to obscure a bright light that appeared to be crossing the mountain and settling over Cold Smoke, one of the largest runs on the ski hill. It was a different kind of light than was typical of the mountain. It looked to her as though the light was hovering, or that it might have actually landed, and she thought she could hear it making a clicking sound. She stood there watching for about five minutes while she rocked her baby to sleep. The object didn't move until a train whizzed by. As if startled by the noise and movement, the light suddenly disappeared. The young woman searched the mountainside, but the light was gone. Thinking nothing more of the sighting, she returned to bed with her baby.

It appeared to be a restless night all around, and about an hour later the baby was once again crying for attention. Returning to the living room, the woman couldn't help but peer outside to see if the light she'd seen earlier was still there—and it was. It was extremely bright, almost white with "an orangey light coming from the centre," and this time it appeared quite animated, darting from place to place quicker than any helicopter or airplane she'd ever seen. Then just as suddenly as it had appeared, it was gone. The entire scene left the woman with an unsettled feeling. Even her cat appeared attentive, with its ears perked and its gaze focused out the window. Thinking *out of sight, out of mind,* she shut the blinds and tried to get whatever sleep she still could.

But closing the blinds did nothing to dispel the memory of what she had just witnessed.

Based in the neighbouring town of Houston, where a long string of UFO sightings had been reported over the years, Brian Vike received a call from the unnamed woman the following morning. "She mentioned to me that her husband thought she was seeing things, but it sounds like she was certainly witnessing something rather strange," Vike reported on his website.

In an effort to exclude all the obvious factors that might have caused the unexplained light, Vike called the ski hill management to see if any maintenance work had been done on the runs at that time of the morning. He was told that four of the runs were undergoing some routine maintenance that may have been conducted around that time; however, the position of the light and the description of its erratic behaviour as provided by the witness didn't really match up to the information given by the ski hill management. As well, the witness remembered seeing the bright light travelling a distance of about 3 kilometres, passing over rough terrain, before coming to a stop. Maintenance equipment wouldn't be able to skip across rough terrain, so it wasn't likely responsible for the light.

In the end, Vike determined that whatever the young mother thought she had seen wasn't the result of any grooming equipment, which operates in a predictable, routine fashion. Besides, most folks who live in Smithers are used to seeing such equipment on the mountain and can easily recognize the machines. As far as the woman was concerned, the light she witnessed hadn't behaved in any fashion she'd ever seen before.

"I have determined that this sighting is an unexplained [one]," Vike said at the conclusion of his report.

Unidentified flying objects are not uncommon sights in northwestern British Columbia, but these sightings don't necessarily make it into an official RCMP report. For many years Vike has acted as the region's specialist in the area of unexplained phenomena, which included pretty much everything from UFO to Sasquatch sightings, and residents frequently turned to him to report any strange occurrences.

In the summer of 2002, a series of unusual sightings didn't attract only Vike's attention; it made the local paper.

The August 7, 2002, edition of *The Interior News* ran a story about a sighting reported by Telkwa resident Gordon Stewart. The farmer was watching a movie on July 29 and unwinding from a long day at work when he noticed a strange light shoot across the Telkwa Range, which he can clearly see through his living room window. The light appeared to radiate from a rather large object. From his vantage point, Stewart thought the unexplained entity was about the size of a pickup truck, but because it was quite a distance away, he reasoned it was probably closer to the size of a school bus. The unidentified object didn't make a sound as it passed by, and even when it was in clear view of Stewart's home, the family's dogs—who were outside at the time—didn't seem to react in any way to its presence.

The light was so shocking in its shape, intensity and behaviour that Stewart called the RCMP. After filing a report, Stewart woke his wife, Joanna, who had retired earlier that night, to tell her about what he'd just seen. Startled by what her husband described, Joanna told him that it sounded like something she'd witnessed in the same general direction a couple of months earlier.

A 40-minute drive east of Telkwa along the Yellowhead Highway is the town of Houston. That same July night, not long before Stewart noticed the light from his window, a Canfor employee had witnessed "a phosphorescent-like white ball of light with yellow undertones, which appeared to hover, before slowly crawling across the sky line." According to one newspaper account, the primary witness called over two of his co-workers who also "caught sight of the glowing light, which grew a tail as it gained momentum…. They watched it for 30 seconds as it was dropping in altitude, heading towards Tweedsmuir Park in a southwesterly direction."

Although the Canfor worker called over his colleagues because he wanted someone to collaborate his story, and reassure him that he "wasn't crazy," he asked the newspaper to protect his identity and withhold his name from the public. Stewart, on the other hand, was thrilled to find out someone else had witnessed something that night.

A follow-up story in *The Interior News* further supported Stewart's sighting with additional witnesses who likely saw the same thing. In the August 14, 2002, edition of the paper, a retired schoolteacher living in Quick, a small hamlet located between Telkwa and Houston on Highway 16, reported seeing something unfamiliar that night. She and her son were both outside, near the family's greenhouse, when her son "gave a great yell." Turning to see what had happened, the unnamed woman pointed her flashlight in her son's direction. That's when she saw a strange, glowing oval-shaped object flying quite low to the ground. "I couldn't move. I was in shock," she told reporters.

"The UFO would be like if you took a round circle and started to stretch it out."

A few months earlier, more sightings of weird flying objects had been reported, and again they came from a variety of sources. At around 10:00 PM on February 1, 2002, a man driving home after renting a video at the Smithers Hollywood Video store noticed a glowing object gliding across the sky. He pulled his car over to the side of the road and watched the strange light for a time before continuing home.

That same night, three women reported seeing a "very bright light glowing through the overcast" when they were travelling from Smithers back to their homes in Houston at around 8:45 PM. The moon has a habit of glowing through the clouds—if you've ever been to the area, you'll understand that cloud cover is typical, and sometimes it seems as though the clouds are touching the mountaintops and enclosing the entire Bulkley Valley. But these women soon recognized that this light was different. For one thing, it was moving. Suddenly, the light swooped below the clouds and looked like it was falling to the ground.

An alien presence wasn't the first explanation that popped to mind. Instead, one of the women worried that the light might be a bomb. The women watched as the light continued moving toward the highway, dropping so low it looked like it was skimming the treetops. The closer it came, the larger it appeared. Soon, the light seemed to hover above the car the women were in, which further frightened them but at the same time gave them a clear view of the source of the light they had seen.

There was no doubt in the women's minds that the light was some kind of large craft. As the driver of the car pushed hard on the gas pedal, the backseat passenger was getting a good look at the craft. According to one report, the witness described it as "similar to a boomerang in shape and a 'guesstimate' of size would have placed the object at least 450 feet [135 metres] in length." She also counted "seven large, bright, white lights" with "two orange lights at either end." As the three women sped east toward Houston, the craft appeared to lose interest in the vehicle and moved west toward Telkwa.

A couple of days later, another sighting was reported to local authorities. This time a couple from Houston reported witnessing a "large, bright, white object shooting beams of light down towards the river while hovering at treetop level." And on Valentine's Day, another man reported "something very strange in the night sky" near François Lake, a community east of Houston.

Reports continued to pepper various authorities that winter and into spring. Stewart had no reason to worry that going on record with what he saw would raise eyebrows among his friends and family. By the time Stewart reported his sighting in July 2002 more than 70 "unidentified sightings" had been reported in the north that calendar year alone. Some were glowing lights while others were dish- or cigar-shaped objects. In an area where residents are familiar with typical astronomical events such as northern lights and shooting stars, which regularly light up the night sky, so many reports of celestial anomalies is significant, and Vike has recorded every one of those sightings. "There is so much going on here it's nuts," Vike told *The Interior News*.

A Little Farther West

One of the earliest sightings that made it into an official file coming out of Smithers occurred on the night of October 21, 1980. This strange light didn't lend itself to an explanation that could be dealt out in a clean, neat package, but officials certainly tried to explain it away.

Bob Walker was getting ready to go to work around 7:30 that Tuesday evening. He was scheduled to teach a class at one of the local schools in town, and he was admittedly a little preoccupied thinking about the evening's lesson plan as he waited for a taxi. But when he hopped into the car and settled into the back seat, taxi driver Rita David appeared somewhat animated. She didn't immediately drive Walker to his destination. Instead, she asked him to take a look outside. In particular, she was pointing to a bright light that she told reporters hovered or flew "over the ridge area directly to the south of town" near one of the lifts under construction on the ski hill. Walker later described the light as being "a circular shape and a stronger light than what is normally seen as a street light or even a star or a satellite." The light was darting erratically back and forth over the ridge and toward Hudson Bay Mountain, and after watching it move around for about five minutes, Walker decided his wife, Diane, needed to see the strange sight. Calling her outside, he pointed to the light and asked her to take note of what happened, and with that he left for work.

For the next 45 minutes Diane watched the light, which she described as a circular-shaped "bright flashing white light" surrounded by a "bright pink glow," as it rapidly darted back and forth along the ridge. For a while it hovered over the mountain's peak and looked to Diane like it was almost "using the mountain top as a sort of central point." Suddenly the light jutted toward town, then back up the mountain again, and it repeated that back-and-forth action for a time.

Diane went into the house for a few minutes, and when she came back outside, the object was gone. It didn't appear again that night. When Walker returned home from teaching his class, the couple called the RCMP to report their sighting. By that time, it was about 9:45 PM.

Constable James B. Colville of the Smithers RCMP detachment visited the Walkers at their home shortly after the couple called in their sighting—it doesn't take more than a few moments to get from one corner of the community to another. Walker repeated his story, which didn't waver from their brief conversation on the phone, but Colville wondered why the couple hadn't called in their sighting at any time during the 45 minutes the object was apparently in the sky. Bob said he didn't call initially because he thought no one would take him seriously, but the more he thought about it, the more he became convinced that filing a report was necessary. Also, he'd had a class to teach. It was one thing for students to contrive far-fetched reasons why their assignments might be late and quite another for the teacher to say he was tardy getting to class because he was busy reporting a UFO sighting.

As the interview progressed, Colville learned that the sighting had occurred some time between 7:30 and 8:30 PM; all three witnesses confirmed that fact. They also agreed on the description of the object, as well as its unique behaviour. According to Colville's report, the UFO was circular when it was stationary, but it was more of an "inverted dish-like shape" when moving." The light and its intensity changed depending on its movements, as well. It always glowed a bright white, but when it wasn't moving, the object had a bright white light around the lower portion of its sphere, and it lit up the mountain side with a pinkish glow. Walker also guessed the craft hovered between 1525 and 1980 metres in the air, and darted about rapidly and unpredictably, faster than any plane or helicopter he had ever seen.

Colville observed Walker and his wife while they shared their story. He noticed that Walker appeared "very calm and very collected" as he relayed the incident. Diane, on the other hand, was excited and animated. Still, the couple didn't look as though they'd been drinking that night, and Colville noted in his report that neither of them "had any odour of alcohol on their breath whatsoever."

Standing in the Walker's living room, Colville had a clear view of Hudson Bay Mountain—there wasn't even a streetlight interrupting the scene. For a change, the sky was clear, and "the moon [cast] a light down on the snow of the ridge." If it had been Colville standing in that living room that night and witnessing the strange event, he might have found himself just as confused about what he'd seen as the Walkers were.

Colville bid the Walkers good night and drove his cruiser down First Street to Rita David's residence on King Street and Third Avenue. Unfortunately, Rita wasn't home and Colville had to content himself with speaking to her on the phone. Again, the Walkers' story was reiterated almost verbatim. Rita agreed that she'd been the first to witness the strange sight, and that she pointed it out to Walker. Although Colville didn't have the opportunity to talk to Rita in person and watch her reaction to his interrogation, he noted that "she sounded to me at that time to be sober and completely believable."

The evening was turning into a quest to solve a mystery that Colville likely thought might end up without any answers. It was now 10:50 PM, and Colville took his investigation to the Smithers Airport. He was hoping to speak with Bruce Bobick, the terminal dispatcher on duty at the time. Perhaps Bobick could clear up the conundrum with some information about a helicopter or weather balloon or anything concrete. But Bobick had nothing to add to the investigation. The last plane of the evening departed from the Smithers Airport at 7:00 PM, and the airport wasn't equipped with a radar tracking device at the time. Comox or Prince George were the nearest facilities with this kind of specialized equipment, Bobick told Colville. The officer would have to contact one or both of the facilities if he was going to find the information he was looking for.

Colville's report closes on a somewhat frustrating note. His attempts to get any information from the Comox Armed Forces Base came to a dead end. The woman answering the phone at the base took down all his information, including many of the details involved in the sighting, but she wouldn't confirm whether an officer would return Colville's call or not.

As far as Colville was concerned, the Walkers and Rita David were credible witnesses. The officer noted that although some development was going on at the ski hill, and a road did wind its way up the mountain, neither situation seemed to provide a reasonable explanation for the sighting. For one thing, trees obscure the road and even a vehicle driving with its high beams on would likely proceed up the mountain unnoticed. He also discarded the idea that any construction on the ski hill might be responsible for creating the strange glow in the sky. According to his report, "the complainants stated that this object was not coming from within the tree area or on the mountain itself, but flying above the ridge and also the three peaks of the Hudson Bay Mountain."

Deciding he'd done all he could to investigate the sighting, Colville forwarded the report, along with the information he'd collected, to his superiors in Prince Rupert and closed the file "until such time as correspondence is received to re-open [it]."

A satisfactory answer was never found, and the story the Walkers and Rita David undoubtedly shared with their family and friends settled into the annals of Bulkley Valley folklore.

Turning Back the Clock

Strange sightings in the sky aren't strictly a recent occurrence in the Bulkley-Nechako region of the northwest, which encompasses the area from Smithers to Vanderhoof. They've occurred throughout history and have been recorded for decades. However, in the early days of these sightings, logical theories about what the objects might be were often reached even in the absence of any concrete supporting evidence.

On April 29, 1959, the northwest experienced an explosion of sightings. It was a bright flash in the sky that first captured the attention of witnesses in Houston. That flash sent something spiralling to the ground, leaving a trail of grey-blue smoke behind it. From RCMP reports about the event, the sightings in Houston were considered the first sighting location, and the farthest west.

Observers in Southbank, a little farther east on Fraser Lake, saw what they described as a "fireball trailing smoke or vapour...from east to west or northwest at a high altitude." They saw a blast first, then heard a delayed explosion.

The description of a "grey-blue" trail of smoke continued when witnesses from Burns Lake and the surrounding area reported a loud explosion. They heard a blast first, which was followed by a "puff of smoke curling within itself," and some of the witnesses from this location claimed they heard what sounded like a "jet aircraft just before the explosion."

Moving farther east, witnesses in Endako described the cloud of smoke as a "blue and purple cloud forming in the northwest." They too mentioned an explosion, followed by something that sounded like a jet "breaking the sound barrier." They also described the expulsion of some kind of "black object" that "[fell] into the clouds" after the explosion. The cloud of smoke hung in the air for about 10 minutes.

Residents claiming to have seen this anomaly were so numerous that officers investigating the case kept moving east along the Yellowhead Highway and had no problems finding observers in community after community. In Fraser Lake a lingering smoke trail was noticed in the sky, forming a "partial loop" that one witness described as the letter "C." Observers in this community didn't remember hearing an explosion, but witnesses farther east heard one. They also recalled a "blue and black cloud" that formed shortly after the explosion, and a "fire ball [that] descended to the horizon."

By this point in the investigation, officers had identified as many as 30 witnesses spanning an east-to-west distance of almost 70 kilometres who had all seen the unexplained aerial event unassisted, as in without the use of binoculars or any other visual aids. Their testimony was obtained independent of one another, and their stories were consistent.

That something happened that spring day in 1959 was never doubted; exactly what appeared in the sky and exploded was still up to debate. R. Schmidt, the lead investigator in the case, had determined there was "no air traffic in the area at the time of the sighting." He'd transcribed and collated every witness' description outlining what had happened and summarized that series of events into a concise outline. But he was unable to identify the object or explain why it had exploded. He also wasn't able to locate a single witness "north of the suspected flight path" he reasoned the object had taken.

And if something had actually exploded, why had no one come forward with any bits or pieces of wreckage? Surely an event of that magnitude would have produced some debris.

In his final report to the Air Defence Command of the RCAF, located in St. Hubert, Québec, Schmidt suggested the object involved in the explosion might have been a meteorite that had penetrated the earth's atmosphere. He went on to suggest that those bits that hadn't immediately burnt up probably fell to the earth. In the absence of proof backing this theory, those who witnessed the explosion and residents throughout the northwest were left wondering.

Once again, as far as the authorities were concerned, the case was closed.

Alaska Highway: A Stunning Show

Silently, one by one, in the infinite meadows of heaven,
Blossomed the lovely stars, the forget-me-nots of the
angels.

–Henry Wadsworth Longfellow, American poet,
from his poem "Evangeline"

The narrow, curvy, two-lane asphalt road connecting
Dawson Creek, BC, to Alaska's Delta Junction is
a challenging drive. For the most part, it has no
shoulders and no ditch—just a sheer drop into
a valley below. Gas stations and food and lodging
opportunities dot the route every 30 to 80 kilometres
or so, providing motorists with a somewhat regular
opportunity to fuel up, but in winter, those services
are considerably reduced. When you see a gas station,
you fuel up regardless of whether you're running on
empty or not. Years ago, this long stretch of highway
was even more remote, especially in the winter months.

Proposals for the construction of the 2237-kilometre
stretch of road known as the Alaska Highway began
in the 1920s with a dream of connecting the U.S. to
Canada and Russia. It took the better part of two decades
before sod was turned on the project, on March 8,
1942, but the roadwork accelerated considerably as
World War II continued to escalate. On October 28
of the same year, the route was complete, and the
highway was officially dedicated on November 20.

Residents living in Canada's north now had a solid link to the rest of their country, lessening the sense of isolation often experienced in remote areas.

The Alaska Highway also opened up the north to a new industry. Drawn by the beauty and history of the land, visitors began to flock to the region, and tourism developed into a main economic force. Wilderness pursuits such as big-game hunting and fishing became so popular that in 1966, the Guide Outfitters Association of British Columbia was established to help non-residents and city dwellers safely manoeuvre their way through the bush.

Although a resident of the historic Lower Mainland community of Cloverdale, which is now part of the Greater Vancouver area, D. Oldershaw knew his way around the bush. In December 1967, the assistant provincial apiarist was spending a few days with Dal Meservy and his brother, J. Meservy, hunting in the northern wilderness along the Alaska Highway. At about 6:45 on the morning of December 14, the men were warming themselves with cups of coffee and gazing north across two mountain ranges and their subsequent meadows. The hunters were enjoying their beautiful surroundings while waiting for the sun to rise so they could set out on their day's journey. It was at that point that Oldershaw noticed a bright light.

At first, Oldershaw thought it was a star. But it was bright, far outshining any of the other stars on that clear early morning, so clear that he couldn't help but point it out to his companions:

...it moved a short distance in a straight line flight in a westerly direction, then stopped. (The movement had no acceleration or deceleration, just fast travel between two points.) The position in relation to our view was now at two o'clock and its altitude approximately 4000 feet [1.2 kilometres]. *It remained perfectly still for one full minute, then dropped like a meteor a distance of some 3500 feet* [one kilometre], *in a southwesterly direction, then stopped abruptly.*

Assessing the light's location by observing the tree-lined ridges in front of him, Oldershaw estimated the object was somewhere between the two ranges, about 4 kilometres away from where they were sitting. And the light was changing shape; Oldershaw now thought it looked about "the size of a 3/8 of an inch disc [95 millimetres] of alternating (changing colours) radiant light."

According to Oldershaw's description, the light continued to move, darting rapidly from one direction to another, sometimes vertically and on occasion horizontally, until it came to a sudden stop, hanging as if it were "sitting in space on a gigantic unseen tripod." At some point while the light was stationary, Dal Meservy flashed the headlights of his car. The action seemed to stimulate a response, and the light suddenly moved toward the men, stopping about 1.5 kilometres from their position.

[The object] *became stationary and remained so long enough for us to really note with some detail the nature of the light emitted. There were two distinct phases of the light—one being a very pure pale green as produced by an expensive light filter of very precise frequency, while the other was a very bright transparent white light of adamantine lustre.*

The hunters continued to observe the unidentified object, which constantly alternated between the two distinct phases of light Oldershaw described. Then suddenly it darted north, disappearing within seconds.

That the three men corroborated one another's story about the unexplained light gave a certain amount of credibility to the letter Oldershaw penned to the UFO Reports Branch of the Radio and Electrical Engineering Department of the Montréal Research Council on January 10, 1968.

Other strong components of Oldershaw's report were the particulars he provided, which were calculated by using known markings. Aside from the verbal description of the light and its actions, Oldershaw also gave other precise details. He stated that the sighting took place between 6:45 and 6:53 AM on Sunday, December 14, 1967, and he noted the exact degrees of longitude and latitude. Oldershaw believed the sighting took place at an altitude of 762 metres, and the temperature at the time was –28°C.

Oldershaw further highlighted what he considered were the "points of scientific interest" with regard to the sighting. In particular, he noted that every time the object moved, it did so in a straight line, reminding him of a hummingbird in flight. The brightness of the light never changed, nor did the direction in which the light shone. To Oldershaw's way of thinking, this excluded the possibility that he was watching a plane. He never saw a "form," and none of the men heard any sounds emanating from the object.

Additionally, Oldershaw's personal credentials were impressive. Not only was he an experienced photographer with keen observation skills, but he was also learned in the field of optics previous to joining the staff of BC's Department of Agriculture. As he explained in his letter, Oldershaw was schooled in the art of "critical observation as to focus [and] structure...of objects."

Clearly, Oldershaw was no ordinary witness. The question that remained was whether he had observed a show provided by Mother Nature or something far more complicated.

It took less than two weeks before Peter Millman, head of the Upper Atmosphere Research Department of the National Research Council, responded to Oldershaw's report. The one-page letter doesn't really offer a concrete answer; in fact, Millman said he couldn't make any definitive statement because he could not "recover some of the quantitative measurements." He did, however, provide what he seemed to believe was a logical theory:

The nature of what you saw most closely resembles the phenomenon observed when a star image is modified by peculiar and unusual conditions in our atmosphere. The results of such action may be quite spectacular, producing rapid motion of the image including changes of shape and colour. While I cannot be certain that this is the explanation of what you saw, this seems to fit best with the nature of your observation.

In fewer than 100 words, Millman basically dismissed the case. Oldershaw was told the "clear and detailed account" of his sighting would be kept on file, but as far as any public documents reveal, it doesn't appear that Oldershaw's sighting merited any further investigation.

If you've ever visited Canada's northernmost regions, you know that the night sky is regularly lit by an abundance of stars. Whether they're simply hanging there, shooting across the sky or being birthed out of massive stellar explosions, so many celestial bodies light up the sky that anyone travelling along the dark highways doesn't really miss the absence of streetlights. Add to that the kaleidoscope of colour displayed by the Aurora Borealis, and the suggestion that what Oldershaw and his companions saw was a natural phenomenon might be a reasonable one.

However, because no further investigation was conducted, it's a safe bet that we'll never really know what was seen that day.

Alexis Creek: Nature's Wonders or Human Ruse?

The most beautiful thing we can experience is the mysterious. It is the source of all true art and all science. He to whom this emotion is a stranger, who can no longer pause to wonder and stand rapt in awe, is as good as dead: his eyes are closed.

–Albert Einstein, German-born theoretical physicist

Wide plateaus and mountain peaks. Fjord-like lakes and lush valleys richly carpeted with wildflowers. Hidden lakes that mirror a crisp blue sky. The endless expanse of wilderness that makes up the Chilcotin District is nothing short of stunning. Located in the West Central Interior of British Columbia, this part of the province is home to large populations of wildlife, but the human population in the area is sparse. It takes a special kind of person to embrace the rugged surroundings and call this corner of Canada home. And the people who do live there are a unique breed all their own.

The Chilcotin First Nations people, who took their name, which means "people of the red ochre river," from the Chilcotin River, were the first inhabitants to settle in the region. But over the years, the peaceful forests and untouched hinterland have attracted adventurous nature lovers from all over the world.

Small-scale ranchers and enterprising business people also provide a backcountry experience for visitors to the area.

Living in this kind of breathtaking environment is invigorating. But it's also somewhat isolating. Alexis Creek is one of the larger settlements, and it's home to only 300 people. The nearest service centre to the community is Williams Lake, 112 kilometres east along the Bella Coola Highway. Because the village is so remote, its residents and those throughout the region all the way to Bella Coola rely on one another—they have to in order to survive. So when a strange object whistled through the air at great rates of speed around 3:00 PM on November 2, 1962, many people noticed.

An unknown object rocketing across the sky would have been a frightening sight at any time, but this was especially true in the later months of 1962 when the world was in the middle of the Cuban Missile Crisis—a period in history that brought the Cold War to a climax, and the possibility of a nuclear conflict seemed imminent. And when that object looked like it was disintegrating in mid-air, and burst into flames before hitting the ground with a loud explosion, that concern increased as dramatically as the scene itself.

The names of most witnesses in the documents surrounding the November 2 "intelligence sighting," and the strange sightings that followed, were blacked out to protect the privacy of the individuals filing reports. But the sheer volume of calls to the RCMP and officials at RCAF Station Puntzi Mountain— a General Surveillance Radar station operated by the North American Aerospace Defense Command (NORAD)—gave the sightings credibility and made them a cause for concern. Of course, there was always the possibility that the object in question was nothing more than a meteor. However, if it was a missile or debris from a satellite, the authorities would be remiss if they didn't conduct an extensive and immediate investigation.

The other consideration was the human factor. Residents of small communities talk, and with so many witnesses reporting what happened that day, it wasn't long before everyone knew the story. The people living in and around Alexis Creek were obviously alarmed, and the overall level of public concern added another sense of urgency to the investigation.

A woman living 13 kilometres west of Alexis Creek appears to have been the first to witness the object whizzing overhead. It was about 2:40 PM. Mrs. K.A. Telford was standing by the garage of her new house. She was talking with her carpenter and facing in a northerly direction when she noticed what she first thought looked like a plane in the sky. But as the airborne object grew near her, she realized it didn't have wings. "I could see a wide band circling the front of the object," she said in her official statement to Corporal P.J. Humphreys of the Alexis Creek Detachment. "As it got broadside to me, I could still see the band."

Telford described the object as smooth, "highly polished" and wider in the front than it was in the back. It was flying low and fast when she saw it, clearing "the trees on the hill behind the house with just a little [room] to spare." As it passed by, she could see "burning particles falling off the back, and when it passed, I could see the fire at the back end of it." Depending on the angle at any given time, Telford thought the object looked "like a rocket in flight" or a large propane tank. It took a few minutes for the object to pass out of sight and disappear behind a hill. Seconds later, the woman heard a loud explosion, followed by a rumbling.

Because most witnesses who report sightings of UFOs that are never explained say they didn't hear a sound, the noise the vessel made added extra concern. Could it be that the "long cylindrical object" Telford watched crumble in mid-air and burst into flames was an attack missile?

It comforted Telford to know she'd shared this sighting with her carpenter. He too had seen the object and heard the explosion it made. Had she been alone when she spotted the craft, she might have thought twice about calling the authorities. A second witness by her side was all the assurance Telford needed to contact the RCMP. Unfortunately, the members on duty at the small detachment were busy with other investigations and didn't get back to her until later that day. But when Corporal P.J. Humphreys filed the initial report with the senior detachment in Kamloops, officials ordered a full investigation into the incident.

Shortly after Telford called to report what she and her carpenter had seen that afternoon, other witnesses began calling in.

Thirty-six kilometres east of Alexis Creek, a full 48 kilometres or more from the vantage point held by the woman and her carpenter, Kurt and Heinz Krause, two highway employees working on the road, saw something strange zooming overhead. Two loggers travelling the highway at that time, as well as a rancher named William Mulbahill, who lived in the Chezacut wilderness, also shared what they saw that day. According to one source, Mulbahill was "standing on his haystack when he heard an explosion. He looked around for the cause of the explosion and saw a bright light on the mountains by Tatlayoko Lake." The rancher thought the "light burnt for approximately 10 minutes" before it gradually disappeared.

Other witnesses to the event, including two men who were standing outside chatting and a woman on horseback riding near Tatla Lake, supported Mulbahill's story. The woman told investigators that when she saw the light, it looked to be travelling in a southwest to northeast direction, and by that point was moving slower than other witnesses had reported.

She described it as "a welding light, without the blueness," and from her position, the "object did not appear to be changing course or losing or gaining altitude." It did, however, look like it was "dropping various size pieces from the back of it and did not make noise until 2 or 3 minutes after it passed and then there was a series of explosions." As the RCMP pieced these and other reports together, officials estimated the explosion could be heard within a 112-kilometre radius.

That a missile or aircraft had invaded the otherwise peaceful wilderness of the Chilcotin District was a possibility, so investigators turned their inquiry to the USAF at Puntzi Mountain Air Force Station. Officers were wondering if the radar facility had picked up any aircraft in the area at the time of the sightings. It had not. Officers then inquired whether the RCAF and USAF Sector Command at McCord Field and Rescue Coordination Centre in Vancouver had recorded signs of any aircraft in the area. Again, the answer was no.

Major R.A. Wigen, commanding officer at the Puntzi station at that time, had a suggestion for the investigating officers. After discussing the RCMP reports with some of his colleagues, Wigen strongly suggested the sightings were most likely the result of a meteor bursting through the atmosphere. In this case, Wigen posited the theory that on entering the earth's atmosphere, the meteorite had heated up and become a fireball, bursting into pieces as it travelled and eventually hitting the earth.

Wigen wasn't the only one convinced that the subject of much investigation was nothing more than a meteorite. On November 7, Superintendent J.B. Harris of the Kamloops Subdivision RCMP issued a news release stating that "the object that sped through the sky and crashed onto the face of Mount Razorback in the Chilcotin Country" was possibly a meteorite. He went on to say that although the RCMP dispatched "one of their aircraft" to the area, turbulent weather prevented the pilot from getting closer than a kilometre or so to the mountainside. Spotting anything of value to help determine what might have happened, especially in light of the fresh fall of snow, was impossible.

However, an obvious burn on the mountainside seemed to close the case as far as Harris was concerned. "No planes have been reported missing. There is nothing to indicate people are involved so it's out of our hands," he stated. Wing Commander Biden, head of Mount Lolo Radar Base, didn't appear to agree with Harris' conclusion. "It's something that can not be disregarded," he said. "It's been reported to head-quarters and I've requested an investigation."

It was clear that investigators had several angles to pursue to adequately cover all the bases. They first explored the possibility that construction work in the area might have required the use of explosives, but investigators quickly discounted that idea. The meteorite theory was certainly worthy of consideration, so the officers contacted Dr. W.F. Slawson, a specialist at the Institute of Earth Scientists, which at the time was located at the University of British Columbia in Vancouver. Before making a determination on Wigen's theory, Slawson travelled to Alexis Creek on November 11 and interviewed the witnesses himself. Unfortunately, the weather prevented Slawson from searching the area where observers believed the object had finally landed.

Meanwhile, two hunters scoping out the Skinner Mountain area noticed a "cone object" during their travels around November 5. Not sure what they'd found, and not wanting to be burdened with extra weight during their hunting expedition, the two brothers placed the object beside a tree and left it there with the intention of alerting the authorities to its presence once they returned to town. As it happened, they bumped into Corporal P.J. Humphreys on November 9. The officer was investigating something unrelated to the sightings at the time, but his interest was piqued as soon as he heard the hunters' story. The brothers agreed to reconnect with Humphreys when the officer finished his current task and was able to hike to the location.

Once Humphreys met up with the brothers, it took the trio quite some time to find the strange object, but eventually the hunters spotted it perched beside the tree where they'd left it. Corporal Humphreys described the object and the scene:

> *This object was cone shaped aluminum construction, 13½ inches* [34 centimetres] *at thick end, tapering down to two inches and 36 inches* [91.5 centimetres] *in length. Same had not been in the area very long as there was no mark left on the ground where it was found, whereas, due to the rotten ground surface, it most certainly would have left a mark if it had been there for any length of time.*

Corporal Humphreys brought the odd-looking cone to the detachment. Although the officer couldn't say for certain that the aluminum debris he recovered had anything to do with the mysterious sightings, he showed it to Major Wigen, Captain W. Brown, USAF and Flying Officer Dobie, and as many members of the Puntzi Mountain Air Force Base as possible to see if anyone could identify the object.

The general consensus was that this particular object was a "chaff dispenser," a vessel used to dispense waste material. Wigen agreed to look into its origin, and on November 13 he called Corporal Humphreys with some interesting news. Wigen said their enquiries showed that the "tank and three other tanks had been jettisoned from a CF100 aircraft out of Comox Air Base, on 4-11-62."

The next day, First Lieutenant M. Filyk, of the RCAF Mount Lolo Radar Base in Kamloops, arrived in Alexis Creek and made his own inquiries about the entire investigation. Filyk also called the Comox

Air Base to confirm Wigen's claims. To his surprise, Filyk was told that, "no tanks had been jettisoned over this area, nor anywhere else, and from the description of the tank, it did not appear to be a tank similar to the type used on Canadian aircraft."

The only dumping that officials at Comox would admit to doing involved fuel that had been jettisoned "over their dumping grounds at Comox." Furthermore, they were interested in learning where Wigen had received his erroneous information. Filyk promised he'd try to provide them with an answer to that question.

It seemed that at every step, the investigation was stirring up more questions than answers.

In his report of November 18, Humphreys shared his thoughts on the investigation:

From the information gathered from the various eye-witnesses to the UFO, it is my opinion that this was not a meteor, but rather some type of craft which is under power and controlled. Capt. R.E. Barnes, USAF chief pilot at Puntzi Mountain Air Base, during the early stages of this investigation advanced the theory that this object could have been a booster rocket off a missile. However, from all the conjecture there is in this matter, nothing definite is known regarding this UFO which passed over this area, and unless F/Lt. Filyk is able to come up with any enlightening information in his subsequent investigation, it is thought it will remain a mystery.

For Humphreys and the RCMP in Alexis Creek, as challenging as this mystery was, it was evident they'd have to pull back on their investigation until any additional information came in.

While the active part of the investigation had been discontinued on most fronts by early December 1962, the various authorities were still waiting for the results of the analysis of the chaff collected from the dispenser found by the hunters. Photographs were also taken and sent to various agencies in the hope that the object could be identified.

Regrettably, the reports filed on these items were inconclusive, and the missile-like aircraft that ripped through the sky and smashed into a mountain in the Chilcotin District was never identified. A concrete connection between the aluminum debris discovered by the hunters and the many reported UFO sightings from November 2 was also never made.

In the late 1960s, a Canadian UFO researcher named John Magor investigated stories of UFO sightings and penned several annual reports and newspaper articles on the subject. The 1969 issue of Magor's Canadian UFO Report highlighted a story about a gentleman named Alexander Robertson. According to Magor's report, Robertson was driving his station wagon along the Bella Coola Highway near Alexis Creek with his wife in March 1969 when he noticed "a long metallic object fly across the road in front of him and disappear behind a hill." Interestingly, Robertson echoed Mrs. Telford's description of the 1962 UFO: he said the aircraft could not have been a plane or helicopter because "it had no wings and wasn't making any noise." Robertson continued to explain that right before the vessel disappeared, "it tipped on one side a little, and I thought maybe it was more circular in shape."

Magor also shared the story of another similar sighting that took place during the Christmas season of 1968. This time a resident of Alexis Creek had filed the report. "It was dark on the ground when we saw a tremendous bright green light passing high in level flight in front of us," Alex Whitecross told Magor:

The sun was still shining at that altitude, but this light was self-illuminated. It was as bright as a magnesium flare. I've never seen anything like it, but I'm not saying it was a UFO. I don't believe in them. I just don't know what it was.

Believer or not, Whitecross also denied the possibility that the light he saw could have been a meteor.

Far from the bright lights of civilization, it's possible that at least some of the unidentified sightings witnessed throughout the past century were the results of natural phenomena. It's equally possible that a few of the accounts could have been explained away as being carelessly discarded chaff dispensers or satellite debris falling from the sky.

But for the residents of Chilcotin District, some of the sightings will always defy explanation, and for them, that leaves room for all manner of possibilities.

CHAPTER FOUR

Alberta

The area under the World's First UFO Landing Pad was designated international by the Town of St. Paul as a symbol of our faith that mankind will maintain the outer universe free from national wars and strife. That future travel in space will be safe for all intergalactic beings, all visitors from earth or otherwise are welcome to this territory and to the Town of St. Paul.

–the sign beside the St. Paul, Alberta,
UFO Landing Pad

St. Paul: Out of This World

ABOUT 5600 PEOPLE LIVE in the town of St. Paul, in north-central Alberta. The community is considerably removed from any large neighbouring centre, with the city of Edmonton about 200 kilometres to the southwest and the city of Lloydminster about 115 kilometres to the southeast. Agriculture is the mainstay of the economy for this community, but its business and industrial centre has grown over the years, and the town prides itself in being the major service centre of northeast Alberta. And though it's a long road to get to St. Paul, tourism has blossomed as a major contributor to the local economy, thanks to the town's notoriety as being home to the world's first UFO Landing Pad.

In 1967, Canada was afire with centennial celebrations, and in preparation for our 100th birthday, the Canadian government encouraged communities to embark on special projects to mark the milestone in our nation's history. Centennial parks and arenas and other community amenities were erected throughout the country, but in St. Paul, the focus was on something unique—something foreign. Something alien.

According to St. Paul's Chamber of Commerce, "the basic idea of [building] a landing pad came from Mr. W.R. Treleaven of Hamilton, ON, and Mr. Ken Reed of Calgary, AB." Margo Lagassé, a member of the St. Paul Centennial Committee, argued that such a unique idea would surely raise the interest of anyone who heard of the project.

Organizers saw the structure as something that might draw visitors to the community, especially during a time when the topic of UFOs was of considerable interest to the public.

Stefan Michalak had rocked Manitoba with his first-hand sighting and radioactive soil samples. The Shag Harbour UFO had stumped not only the entire province of Nova Scotia but also the RCMP and Royal Canadian Air Force. And these were just two of the bigger UFO stories of that decade. So St. Paul's council decided that the northern town would earn a world first; the project was a go!

Since then, the whole town has gotten on board with the alien theme. In 1992, a new tourist booth built in the shape of a flying saucer was erected beside the landing pad. And on occasion, local businesses adopted names with alien themes—like UFO Pizza.

But, of course, what would a town with a UFO landing pad do without any UFOs?

When reports of unidentified flying objects trickle in to police headquarters or information lines, a few basic factors must be considered before a lot of man-power and money goes into investigating the sighting. The number of independent witnesses increases the reliability of a sighting.

The authorities also like to make sure the observer hasn't been drinking or otherwise indulging in something that could skew his or her perspective. And of course, if the witness is a prominent member of the community, that usually adds credibility.

So when Constable P.J. Thatcher witnessed a strange aerial occurrence while he was policing the area highways on Christmas evening, 1967, he filed a detailed report right away, which was then forwarded to RCMP headquarters in Ottawa. Thatcher was patrolling Highway 28A near Mallaig, a hamlet north of St. Paul, when he noticed what he thought was a meteor or fireball bursting across the sky at a 40-degree angle. "It appeared to burn up or explode at an angle of about 15 degrees," Thatcher wrote in his report, and it "lit up the sky to almost daylight proportions for approximately 5 to 10 seconds."

Constable Thatcher was a relatively new officer, and although he assumed the event he'd just witnessed was a meteor, he followed to the letter the instructions provided in the "RCMP Operational Manual CO-Air" about how to handle sightings of unknown objects. He reported that the sky was clear, it was 6:11 PM, and there was only a single burst involved in the explosive part of the event, followed by darkness.

The object he saw travelled in an east-west direction and made no sound. As for its size, Thatcher stated that "in comparison to the moon which looks to be the size of a basketball, this would be the size of a golf ball." What captured Thatcher's attention the most was the intensity of the light, and how bright the sky got when the object burst.

Thatcher's superiors must have been satisfied the sighting was that of a meteor, and the matter was forwarded to a Professor R.E. Folinsbee for further study. A little over a month later, on February 7, 1968, a report on what appeared to be another meteor spotted in the area was sent to Dr. I. Halliday of the Stellar Physics Division of the Department of Energy, Mines and Resources. The short, concise telex message listed the meteorite sighting as occurring 8 miles (13 kilometres) north of St. Paul at 6:58 PM on February 5. It, too, lit up the countryside.

With a rich tradition of meteorites hurling through the atmosphere in the St. Paul area, it's no wonder that sightings of strange objects were met with the attitude that they weren't really mysterious—the objects were likely meteors, so no further time or energy was required for an investigation.

Some residents would beg to differ with that reasoning.

Under the "Totally Bizarre" Category

In the late-night hours of Tuesday, March 2, 1971, nine-year-old Milton Crier was fooling around outside his home on Saddle Lake Cree Nation, enjoying the mild weather and a little time on his own. The sky was clear, the air crisp; you could almost feel spring around the corner. It was the kind of night you didn't want to end—the kind of night that reminded you of summer and late-night campfires—and Milton was having a hard time dealing with the idea that he should be thinking about turning in for the night.

But around 10:15, PM that all changed.

It's unclear if it was the cat-like purring sound emanating from the object or the three bright orange and red lights that attracted Milton's attention. But what he was about to see was beyond strange: it was frightening. Without a second thought, Milton rushed into the house yelling "UFO! UFO!" As far as the youngster was concerned, he knew what he'd just witnessed. It was all the encouragement 16-year-old Alice and her 14-year-old brother Herman needed to pry them off the couch and to Milton's side.

Together, the three youngsters watched as a saucer-shaped object rimmed with blinking lights hovered between 1.5 and 3 metres above the treetops lining the nearby fields. The object seemed to almost hang in place for a time before it started to move again, travelling at a speed the three witnesses estimated was about 30 kilometres per hour.

Alice rushed back into the house to wake her parents, hoping they might catch a glimpse of the mysterious object before it disappeared. Mrs. Crier said she looked up and noticed bright blue and orange lights streaming into the bedroom, but they disappeared before she could make it to the window. Just as suddenly as it had appeared, the strange saucer-shaped object darted away in a westerly direction.

The next morning, Albert Crier, the children's father, made a trip to the RCMP station to report what his children had witnessed. The father was really convincing, and after hearing the story, Constable E.F. Lammerts drove out to the reserve to speak with the youngsters.

All three siblings were firm about what they had seen, and each agreed on the details of the story. They said they were about 500 yards (455 metres) away from the hovering craft, and the object was visible for a total of about three minutes.

In his report, Lammerts noted that he'd spent considerable time interviewing the witnesses and believed they were sincere and that "their sighting [was not] a figment of their imagination."

Lammerts also pointed out that the location of the sighting was in direct line with the "flight path of CFB (Canadian Forces Base) Cold Lake" and that a "number of oil rigs surround the area," suggesting that perhaps the three youth were mistaken about what they'd seen and it wasn't a UFO at all.

When presented with the idea that they probably just saw a helicopter, all three witnesses disagreed. They knew what a helicopter looked like—they'd seen helicopters up close before. And what they saw that night was no helicopter.

The sighting was no doubt a life-altering experience for the siblings, especially young Milton. That Constable Lammerts took down their information and treated them with respect and kindness offered a small measure of comfort.

The fact that Lammerts filed a report with the National Resource Council Meteor Centre and his superiors at RCMP headquarters in Edmonton was also reassuring. But despite these and other efforts, no concrete answers were forthcoming. Whatever happened that late night in March 1967 is a question that will probably remain unanswered.

And although the memory of that night might have misted away like the evening fog for the residents of Saddle Lake and anyone who might have taken notice in the surrounding area, for the Crier family, it was an experience they'd never forget.

CHAPTER FIVE

Manitoba

I don't believe in extraterrestrials…but I certainly believe in people's encounters. If someone believes something happened to them, then there is something valid in that, and you have to take it seriously.

–John K. Samson, lead singer of The Weakerthans, in an interview with Brad Frenette, *The National Post*, October 20, 2010

Falcon Lake: One Wild Encounter

STEFAN MICHALAK STOOD TALL, stretched his back to one side and then the other, hoping to loosen the tension in his muscles. He tipped up his hat, wiped his brow with the back of his hand and pulled his topper back over his head. He'd been walking for hours it seemed, stopping now and again to scrape a strip of moss off a slab of granite and examine the glitter of quartz sparkling through the rock. The theory was that the quartz pointed to the possibility that more valuable minerals might be hidden beneath the solid granite rock face of the Precambrian Shield that made up much of this corner of Manitoba. Michalak had heard stories; he knew of several cases where other miners had struck it rich. It was enough to fuel his enthusiasm.

During his tenure as an amateur prospector, he'd found several quartz veins that looked promising, but nothing serious had ever come of them. Michalak glanced over the newest collection of notes he'd entered into his journal that morning. He'd been to Falcon Lake many times, a summer resort community well equipped with several amenities, including a campground, hotel, golf course and cottage community—he knew what he was looking for. And his meticulous jottings made it easy for him to begin each new investigation where he'd previously left off.

The year earlier, the amateur geologist had scoured much of the portion along the southern end of the Whiteshell Provincial Park in search of precious metals, but this was the first time in 1967 that he'd managed the hour-long trip from Winnipeg. For the first five months of the year, the weather had been somewhat inclement. But the forecast for the May long weekend offered a promising break in an unpleasant pattern: according to official weather reports, that Saturday, May 20, would be mostly clear with some broken cloud cover occasionally blocking what otherwise could have been a very hot sun.

Convinced that if he just persisted he'd find what he was looking for, Michalak pushed through the disappointments he'd experienced time after time and, as they say, kept his eye on the prize.

Hopefully he'd strike silver. Maybe nickel. Perhaps, if he could be so bold as to hope, even gold. In 1890, a prospector by the name of Tom Moore was the first to stake a 51-acre claim and open a shaft near Star Lake, just northeast of where Michalak stood at that very moment. Moore's foray into the thick granite foundation of that Manitoba wilderness wasn't profitable. But in 1910, 20 years after Moore's initial claim, George Knudson restaked the property and partnered up with J.H. Hicks of the Penniac Reef Gold Mines Ltd. After three years, the men's hard work finally paid off with the recovery of the equivalent of one gold bar. In 1915 the mine produced enough for a second gold bar. Over the years, samples continued to be tested, and the owners kept the faith that they would eventually hit it big.

Michalak was convinced that persistence was the only thing that separated success from failure. He just had to keep plugging away and eventually he'd find the end of his rainbow.

He hadn't found his pathway to success that morning, but Michalak had spent a pleasant few hours in the rugged Manitoba backcountry. He had all the details of his hard work recorded in his journal to help guide his future endeavours. And thanks to his chipping hammer and measuring tape, he uncovered a rather promising-looking vein of quartz.

All in all, it had been a perfectly peaceful spring morning except, of course, for the rather vocal geese.

The female geese had howled up a storm most of the morning, and the ganders weren't too quiet, either. There had been an ebb and flow to their honking for hours now. Damn if their frenzied cries weren't picking up again.

As Michalak glanced over toward the swamp, he noticed the flock had added quite a display to their noise. Now they were flapping their wings and running across the water in typically unmapped chaos. But from the corner of his eye, Stefan noticed a different sort of flashing in the form of a set of lights. No, there were two. Two separate sets of lights floating in the air and changing colours. The lights were bordering the narrowest part of two disk-like aircraft. Exactly what kind of aircraft they might be was perplexing, though. Michalak had never seen aircraft that looked like that—and he'd seen quite a variety of military and civilian choppers, planes and specialized jets during his stint overseas during World War II. Of course, things had changed since then. There was no stopping progress. No telling what the Americans might have created since Michalak had left the States and moved to Canada.

Whatever these two crafts were, they were getting closer. The engines running these rotating wonders were so silent that if it wasn't for the geese and Michalak's need to stretch, chances were favourable that he wouldn't have noticed them at all. The lights were changing colours. Red. Blue. Even the aircraft themselves seemed to be changing colour. One was hovering about 3 metres or so over the ground, and then just as suddenly as it appeared, it turned and faded back into the clouds; the second aircraft landed about 30 metres away from Michalak's position.

Snatching up his journal and pencil, Michalak started sketching the bolder of the two ships, noting every detail. As with the geological jottings he collected over the years, Michalak left no stone unturned. He used three main lines in making his sketch, with each line delineating 30-centimetre sections. From his vantage point, Michalak thought the craft was about 3.5 metres at its highest point. He estimated the length of the craft at between 10 and 12 metres from its centre to its outer edge. He even noted the direction the crafts came from: 225 degrees south, southwest declination. As for speed—well, it was fast. Mighty fast. Three, four, maybe five times faster than any jet he'd ever seen, but there was no way he'd even guess at an actual number.

The aircraft opened its hatch, giving Michalak more information to include in his sketch. Shades of violet were emanating from the vehicle. Rib-like sections lined the interior of the outer shell, which the prospector estimated were between 45 and 55 centimetres thick. As Michalak was preoccupied with his sketch, he was startled by what sounded like several men talking. If he had taken a moment to evaluate his own reaction, he would have had to admit it was somewhat odd. Most people wouldn't consider it overly cautious to be a little unnerved by the vehicle's presence and the sound of chatter coming from within. Michalak, however, wasn't the least bit fazed.

"If you are Yankee boys, you come out and don't be afraid," Michalak called out. At that point, he was still betting on the idea that the craft was American in origin, and perhaps its pilots had taken a wrong turn or were having some technical difficulties. "I [won't] sell your secret for a lousy green buck…if you need help, just come out."

While Michalak seemed more amazed than afraid of the strange object, the inhabitants of the disk-like craft didn't seem all that confident in his trusting nature to show themselves. According to Michalak, the inhabitants of the craft continued to chatter, so Michalak drew on his extensive repertoire of languages and tried to communicate with the unseen men in German, then Italian, Polish, Ukrainian, even Russian. Clearly he didn't manage to make a linguistic connection because during Michalak's supreme effort to communicate, the hatch began to close without the apparent inhabitants ever acknowledging his presence. How rude, he must have thought. He hadn't even managed to finish asking his questions.

In any case, he didn't have the time to worry about their absence of manners at that moment. He had more important things to do before the ship disappeared completely. He needed to develop an accurate description of the three-part latch that fit together so perfectly that Michalak wasn't able to distinguish where it disappeared into the armoured body once it had closed.

Also, there was something he had to do for himself— a desire that burned almost as hot as the heat radiating from the craft. He just had to touch the air ship before it took off. Stepping closer, Michalak noticed a grill-like feature along its side. Once he got close enough, he reached out and placed his gloved hand against the craft. At that moment, it surged and pulled away, allegedly blasting heat through the grill and burning a replica pattern on his abdomen.

Debilitating pain ripped through Michalak's body. On reflex, he ripped the shirt off his back and pulled the melted, charred glove from his hand. Despite the burning sensation searing through his skin, Michalak fought to maintain his focus and jot down anything else he thought might be of value down the road. He'd have to tell the police about what he'd seen. He'd have to tell an authority somewhere, and he had no doubt they'd want every possible detail. Michalak was alone in the bush. No one else was around to pick up anything he'd missed. Then again, there was no one else around to corroborate his story either.

It was about this time that Michalak doubled over and vomited.

Constable G.A. Solotki was cruising down the highway west of Falcon Beach around 3:00 PM on Saturday, May 20, when he noticed Michalak walking along the south shoulder in the direction of the resort community. Solotki noted that the man looked dishevelled. He wore a "grey cap, brown jacket with no shirt, light coloured trousers, and [was] carrying a brown briefcase." It was an oddly discordant scene: a shabbily dressed fellow walking along in the middle of nowhere, carrying a rather official-looking briefcase. Solotki would soon discover the man's appearance wasn't the most bizarre part of the situation he was about to experience.

As Solotki grew near, Michalak noticed the RCMP cruiser and started flailing his arms in what Solotki could only imagine was an effort to get his attention. The officer pulled his car over in Michalak's direction, but before he had a chance to ask any questions, Michalak started to shout at the patrolman, ordering him to keep his distance. In his report on the encounter, Solotki said that Michalak told him that if he got too close he might "get some sort of skin disease or radiation" from Michalak. Not sure what to make of the situation, Solotki threw a few gentle questions Michalak's way, hoping not to frustrate the obviously upset man any further.

"Can I see some identification?" Solotki asked.

Michalak handed the officer his prospecting papers.

"You look very upset. What seems to be the problem?"

Michalak unloaded his tale in short order, making sure to include details about the two "spaceships" he'd seen, complete with red, glowing lights and the extreme speed with which the aircraft arrived and departed. He also told Solotki about the burns on his stomach, and showed him the hat, glove and shirt that were destroyed by the blast of heat.

"You need medical attention," Solotki said, trying to keep his voice calm as he took a step toward Michalak. The prospector jumped back, warning the officer again to keep his distance or risk being contaminated by radiation. He pulled open his jacket to show Solotki his stomach, and Solotki couldn't help but think it looked like the strange man had grabbed a handful of ash from a fire pit and smeared it on his skin.

Not sure what to make of Michalak and his story, Solotki considered, for a moment, that the wandering fellow might be suffering from an extreme alcoholic episode. But despite Michalak's bloodshot eyes, the officer couldn't detect the smell of spirits. Michalak also appeared sincere, desperate even to tell his tale. Still, in Solotki's professional opinion, Michalak looked and acted a lot like someone who had "over indulged."

Concerned for the man's welfare, Solotki offered to give Michalak a ride to Falcon Beach and help him seek the medical attention he obviously needed. Michalak declined the offer. The prospector was obviously agitated and somewhat confused, and even though he had no problem unleashing his experience in great detail to the officer, Michalak repeatedly told Solotki to keep his story confidential. Solotki didn't see Michalak as a danger to himself or the public. With nothing left to do, Solotki moved along and left the deranged man alone with his ramblings.

Thirty minutes later, Michalak showed up at the Detachment Office asking for Solotki and looking for a doctor.

"The closest doctor is in Kenora, Ontario—about another hour down the road," Solotki explained, adding that Michalak's other options were to take the bus to Steinbach or Winnipeg. Because the man lived in Winnipeg, it appeared a bus back home was the most logical choice. Whether he was concerned about the possibility of contaminating other passengers with radiation or not, at 8:10 PM, Michalak boarded the westbound bus.

Flanked by his wife and 19-year-old son Mark, Stefan Michalak was sharing his experience at Falcon Lake with Mr. J. Barry Thompson when Constable Zacharias and Constable C.J. Davis arrived at Michalak's home at 314 Lindsay Street. It was Tuesday, May 23. A full three days had passed since Michalak's encounter, and although he was still reeling from its after-effects, Michalak was animated and descriptive, and his story remained consistent. Thompson was hanging on

Michalak's every word, taking copious notes and obviously captivated by what the man had to say.

Zacharias and Davis would soon learn that Thompson was a member and investigator with the Aerial Phenomena Research Organization (APRO), an organization based in Tucson, Arizona. A couple named Jim and Coral Lorenzen started the group back in 1952. From its inception to the time Michalak reported his experience, APRO had gained a considerable reputation in some circles as a leading UFO research organization. In part, APRO earned its reputation because of the sheer number of prestigious scientists associated with the group, including American physicist James E. McDonald and James Albert Harder, an engineering professor at the University of California, Berkeley.

On behalf of APRO, it was Thompson's job to document unique sightings of unidentified aerial phenomena when he was called upon to do so, and Michalak's experience certainly qualified as such. But once the RCMP began their interview with Michalak, Thompson excused himself and left. Either the man had acquired all the information he was looking for or he decided to go through the notes he'd collected and regroup for a second interview once the police had their turn at interrogating the witness. Michalak was now faced with the exhausting task of reiterating, yet again, details surrounding the stressful episode.

For the next two hours Michalak relived his ordeal once again, this time for Zacharias and Davis. During the interrogation it was obvious to Davis, who later typed what eventually amounted to two days worth of interviews and constructed the formal reports on the matter, that Michalak was physically uncomfortable. When asked how he had been holding up over the last few days, the amateur prospector explained that he'd lost a drastic amount of weight since his experience—about 13 pounds (6 kilograms), he estimated. He couldn't eat, and if he tried to eat, whatever he consumed wouldn't stay down.

Michalak told the officers that his head wouldn't stop pounding, and that he had an acrid taste in his mouth that wouldn't go away—a taste that "seemed to go through [his] entire system" and was "like burned wiring or insulation." The man's wife and son also pointed out that an odd kind of odour lingered in the washroom every time Michalak bathed.

Michalak had other symptoms as well, visible, physical symptoms. He explained that he'd acquired considerable burns on his abdomen from the exhaust expelled by the aircraft as it lifted off the ground. Because the burns left a grate-like impression on his chest, they were something more concrete for investigators to hone in on. Michalak pulled open his loose-fitting shirt so the officers could inspect his wounds, but they were still skeptical about what might have caused them.

"Michalak showed us the burns on his abdomen and chest, and there is a large burn that covers an area approximately 30 centimetres in diameter," Davis wrote in his report. "The burn when we saw it on Tuesday was blotchy and with unburned areas inside the burned perimeter area. There was no indication of blistering. It resembled an exceptionally severe sunburn in the one spot."

There was also something about Michalak's behaviour that put Davis and his colleague on alert.

Michalak was very uncomfortable while we were speaking to him and reminded me of a person that had come out of an epiliptic [sic] fit. He seemed somewhat bewildered by everything and was not alert. He moved very carefully any time he moved his body and when I asked him about this he said that his head was aching so badly that it pained him to move.

If Michalak had indeed experienced what he'd claimed, it made perfect sense that he was ill, agitated and confused. If he was fabricating the entire encounter, it might also provide a reason for his behaviour. At that point in the investigation, the two officers were trying to keep an open mind. Stick to the facts—or at least collect the facts as Michalak saw them. And while they were at it, they'd throw in a few of their own additional questions here and there, just to be sure that the man wasn't a con artist trying to pull a fast one on the authorities.

"So, have you seen the doctor?" one of the officers asked Michalak.

Michalak nodded. He said his son had taken him to the Misericordia Hospital's emergency department in Winnipeg, but all Michalak told the intern on duty was that he'd been burned by aircraft exhaust because "[he] felt that if [he] told them what really happened [he] would not be believed and they would think that [he] had lost [his] mind." His reasoning made good sense to the officers questioning him at that time.

The thought that Michalak perhaps suffered from mental illness was something both Zacharias and Davis entertained as well; who wouldn't entertain that possibility after hearing the bizarre story Michalak had been sharing? During the course of their investigation, the officers inquired at the Selkirk Mental Hospital, the Brandon Mental Hospital and the Winnipeg Psychiatric Institution to see if Michalak had ever been a patient. He had not. Perhaps Michalak had developed a new neurosis, one that hadn't been detected by his family doctor. Surely his employers would know of any new or odd behaviour. But a quick consultation with the administration at Inland Cement, where Michalak had worked as an industrial mechanic for the previous six years, suggested he was the hard-working, reliable, family-centred individual he claimed to be.

Furthermore, Michalak said that he had scoffed at reports he'd heard of UFO sightings in the Falcon Lake area in the past, stories he'd read in newspapers and magazines. Michalak said he thought those earlier reports were bogus, and the claimants were nothing but crackpots. Now Michalak was faced with the realization that he too had seen something he couldn't logically explain, and he didn't want to be considered a crackpot by his friends and family—or by strangers who didn't even know him. That's why he didn't want the public to know about his encounter, and why he told Solotki to keep his story confidential.

Michalak said he had another reason for being secretive, too. He was sure he'd discovered a "good nickel strike in the area." Too much attention to his story would surely attract the more inquisitive adventurers to the Falcon Lake area to check out the site for themselves. If there was just one amateur prospector among that demographic—and the Whiteshell Provincial Park area attracted a large number of geologists and prospectors drawing core samples from the granite slabs that set the foundation for much of the forest floor—that individual might stumble upon the nickel Michalak said he'd found.

All this sounded plausible, but there was one large flaw in the reasons Michalak gave for his apparent reluctance to say too much to too many people. By the time Davis and his colleague met with the man at his Winnipeg home, Michalak had shared his story—and in a big way. He'd contacted the media about his Falcon Lake encounter. In fact, when Davis asked how the press got the scoop on what was soon to be coined the "Falcon Lake Incident," Michalak said he had called the *Winnipeg Tribune*, one of that city's two major dailies at the time, before he left Falcon Lake the Saturday of the sighting.

Davis asked Michalak why he would do such a thing, especially when he had been so adamant that Officer Solotki keep the story confidential. Michalak said he called the *Tribune* to see if it could do anything for him after he got no satisfaction from speaking with Solotki, though he wasn't specific about what he wanted from the officer. This winding path of peculiar reasoning certainly didn't ring true as far as Davis and just about any other member of the RCMP were concerned. Still, experiencing something as traumatic as Michalak claimed he'd experienced would certainly propel even the most steadfast character into making a few rash decisions.

During that first meeting, Davis and Zacharias conducted an informal interview; the more detailed question-and-answer format would follow on day two of the three-day visit with Michalak. For now, the officers just wanted to get to know Stefan on a casual level; they wanted to build a solid foundation of trust with the man.

Michalak seemed to respond positively to their interest. He showed the officers the undershirt he ripped off his back and subsequently stomped on the ground after it had been burned by the flash of exhaust. He explained how the burning shirt had initially caused a small fire on the moss and lichen clinging to the same rock face where Michalak had, moments earlier, thought he'd discovered nickel. He told the officers he'd put out the fire and then, perhaps with a concern for the environment that wasn't always popular in the 1960s, he said he tossed the dirty, burned shirt into his briefcase. Both Davis and Zacharias spent some time examining the shirt and agreed they noticed an odd smell, "like burned electrical wiring or insulation."

In his official report, Davis described Michalak's actions:

> *...He was wearing a nylon ski-type cap at the time he encountered this object in the bush and was also wearing grinder's goggles to chip rock, to protect his eyes. He had his cap on backwards and the front part of his cap (the part facing the front which would normally be at the back) was melted in a small area, obviously from the heat. He was also wearing a pair of yellow plastic gloves which have a cloth interior and are covered with plastic on the outside. Mr. Thompson, the APRO man, took one of these gloves, the one which was damaged on the fingers where he claims he touched the vehicle...*

Davis was disturbed to find out that Michalak had given Thompson the burned glove, perhaps the one piece of concrete proof that something otherworldly had actually occurred. The officer was even more perturbed when he learned that shortly after his meeting with Michalak, the man had handed over two other pieces of evidence—the burned shirt and cap—to his family physician, Dr. Oatway. Curious about Michalak's story, Oatway arranged to pass the items on to a Dr. Gillies at the Winnipeg Cancer Research Clinic with the understanding that Gillies would arrange to have the items tested for radioactivity.

Clearly, Michalak's actions were breaking the RCMP's investigative protocol. That fact, coupled with Michalak's reluctance to accompany officials to the site, was making it look like Davis and Zacharias would have their work cut out for them over the next couple of days.

After bidding Michalak goodbye following that first visit, Davis and Zacharias visited Dr. Oatway at his Corydon Avenue office to get the physician's take on his patient. This was long before the time when the Freedom of Information and Protection of Privacy Act limited this kind of personal disclosure, and the officers were able to extract quite a lot of information on Michalak and what Oatway thought about the prospector's situation.

The doctor confirmed that Michalak was his patient and that he had no concerns about the man's mental health. However, Oatway also made it clear that prior to the most current visit, the last time he'd seen Michalak was a full year earlier.

With regards to the "evidence" Michalak had passed on to Oatway, along with samples collected around the burns on his skin, the test results were in: no radioactive material was found. It seemed that when passed by the close scrutiny of several specialists, Michalak's story wasn't holding up well.

Still, the investigation was far from over. The next day, Davis and Zacharias were back at Michalak's home, going over his story in minute detail and learning a little more about his past. The officers learned Michalak was born in Poland, served in the United States Army Occupation Troops during World War II and immigrated to Canada in 1949. Based on the information he had from Solotki's earlier reports and descriptions, Davis suspected Michalak might have studied prospecting or geology on a formal scale, and he asked him if this was the case.

"Yes, I went to Saskatchewan and to prospecting school at La Ronge and started a study on my own and I continue this," Michalak told Davis. "I like it, the land and the terrain, and I continue it."

Davis and Zacharias queried Michalak about every detail surrounding the weekend of May 20. They heard about how Michalak's wife packed him enough sausage, cheese, buns, apples and oranges to feed him for the day he was away. Michalak filled the officers in on the kind of prospecting materials he brought with him: a magnet, raw polished porcelain used to "check...for streak and colour," gloves, goggles, a hatchet and chipping hammer, books and his notes. He brought no change of clothing.

On Friday, May 19, Michalak's son dropped him off at the bus station in Winnipeg, where he boarded the bus at 7:15 PM and arrived at Falcon Beach around 9:30 PM. According to Michalak, he checked into the local hotel, put his belongings into room 13, "studied

[his] books for an hour, an hour and a half," and then went to the motel's coffee shop for a cup of java.

"Did you have anything to drink that night?" Davis asked.

"No, no I didn't," Michalak replied.

"No alcoholic beverages at all?" Davis pushed.

"No," Michalak insisted, adding that he went to bed some time around 10:30 PM. As presented, the timeline didn't add up. Davis didn't push the issue: perhaps Michalak had indilged a little and lost track of time or had indulged enough to completely disorient himself well into the next day.

Once Michalak told his story yet again, Davis asked him to accompany him and several members of the Royal Canadian Air Force on a helicopter ride into the area with the hope of pinpointing exactly where it was that Michalak encountered the strange aircraft. The officers decided to contact Dr. Oatway for his opinion on whether Michalak was able to travel; Dr. Oatway advised against it at that time. Clearly Michalak was still reeling from his experience.

Using maps and aerial photographs of the area, Davis then asked Michalak if he could identify the general vicinity that he'd been exploring. Michalak pointed out where he thought he'd been and told the officers that he'd found an old saw on a rock during his exploration, and that he discarded a shopping bag in his haste to leave the area.

Even though Michalak couldn't accompany the entourage, Zacharias, Davis and a seven-member crew of the RCAF, led by Squadron Leader Paul Bissky, left Winnipeg at 1:00 PM on May 25 and flew to Falcon Lake. Surveying the area from the air, they were unable to find "a burn or some...indication of a landing spot." The crew then touched down at the Falcon Lake Golf Course and conducted a ground exploration of the area. Davis and his colleagues looked for the saw and shopping bag Michalak mentioned in his interview, hoping this would give them some indication that they were moving in the right direction. Nothing was located. At that point the search was postponed until Michalak was well enough to accompany the investigators.

No one was waiting with baited breath that the answers to this intriguing, yet unbelievable, mystery would be forthcoming.

With Michalak still under the weather, the authorities decided to expand their investigation into the story surrounding the man and his chance encounter. Suspecting the prospector had indeed indulged in a few libations, Constable Davis asked members of the Falcon Lake detachment to find out what they could about Michalak's activities the night prior to his hitherto unexplained experience. Constable L.A. Schmalz began the inquiry. His first stop was the hotel where

Michalak spent his Friday night, or more particularly, the hotel bar.

William Hastings, the first bartender interviewed, did not recall having served Michalak, or any man matching his description. But Hastings punched out for the night at 8:00 PM. Michalak had boarded the 7:15 PM bus from Winnipeg, so he wouldn't have arrived at Falcon Lake for at least two hours.

Hastings' replacement, on the other hand, seemed to remember a man matching Michalak's description. That bartender, whose name was blacked out on the official police report, remembered serving the individual five bottles of beer. He went on to explain that the man who matched Michalak's description left the lounge at 9:30 PM after drinking three beer, but returned around 11:00 PM and had two more. When Davis later challenged the bartender about his timeline, he admitted he might have been off slightly, but on seeing Michalak, he positively identified him as the customer he had served.

The bartender also told Schmalz that when Michalak returned to the bar for the second time, he asked his server if he knew of any prospectors working in the area "north of Falcon Beach." The bartender told Michalak that, "many men try their luck." When the authorities asked about Michalak's condition after consuming five beers over the course of the evening, the bartender suggested that Michalak was feeling his drinks. However, what seems to have stood out the most to the bartender was Michalak's confidence that he'd "find something in the bush." After Michalak downed his fifth beer, he left the lounge. Presumably he retired for the night because the staff didn't see him after that time.

At this point, one thing was imminently clear: Michalak hadn't been completely honest with the police. He'd had five beers over the course of the evening before his experience, which might have been enough to make a man of average stature a little tipsy. And even if there was any truth to information collected at a later interview during which one individual suggested Michalak had replaced the beer he'd been drinking with a few Presbyterians—rye whiskey mixed with ginger ale—it wouldn't likely warrant the kind of alcohol-induced episode that would produce delusions well into the following afternoon.

Of course, just because Michalak stopped drinking in the hotel's lounge didn't mean he didn't buy himself a bottle of spirits to take with him to his room. That was certainly a possibility investigators intended to check out. Antje Poldervaart was the maid on duty the morning Michalak checked out. When Constable Schmalz asked her if she'd found any empty liquor bottles in Michalak's room, she said she had not. His room had been clean. Too clean if you asked Poldervaart, who made a point of telling the officer that neither the soap nor the towels in Michalak's room had been used. To cover all possibilities, Schmalz checked with the hotel's off-sales as well as the local liquor store to see if Michalak might have made any purchases. None were found.

Michalak hadn't been altogether truthful, but it didn't look as though he was trying to cover up anything that would completely discredit his state of mind at the time. Something traumatic had happened—or so it seemed to Mrs. Martin Buseck, wife of the owner of the Falcon Hotel. Although Michalak had behaved like an ordinary customer on the evening of May 19, when Mrs. Buseck met him again on the afternoon of May 20, his demeanour was completely different. She couldn't remember the exact time, but that day Michalak approached her looking for a doctor. He appeared somewhat dishevelled and was clutching his jacket against his chest. Mrs. Buseck told him no doctor was available at Falcon Beach until July 1, and that he should contact the RCMP if he needed immediate assistance.

In his report, Schmalz reasoned that it was following this meeting with Mrs. Buseck that Michalak made his way to the detachment and spoke with Constable Solotki. Apparently unsatisfied with the results of that line of inquiry, Michalak returned to the hotel and asked Mrs. Buseck if there was a telephone available. He wanted to call Winnipeg. Mrs. Buseck directed him to a pay phone. It was the last time the two spoke.

Any way investigators looked at it, the bizarre nature of Michalak's story was hard to swallow. If, as Michalak initially asserted, the aircraft he'd encountered was some sort of misguided American vessel that exhibited new technology, surely there would have been other reports of the sighting. The same argument applied if the unidentified flying object defied logical explanation and was in fact some kind of alien spacecraft: someone else, somewhere else, should have seen something, especially given that even the RCMP had acknowledged an "increasing prevalence of UFO sightings and reports" in the area. At that point in the investigation, officers had been unable to corroborate Michalak's account.

Still, if anything, Mrs. Buseck's description of her meeting with Michalak, along with the report penned by Constable Solotki, muddied the waters even more. According to both accounts, the man seemed genuinely distressed. Something out of the ordinary had occurred—or at the very least, Michalak believed he'd experienced something disturbing. This was enough to keep the police involved.

Michalak's story caused considerable debate, and sometimes even fear, among Manitoba residents back in the 1960s. The incident made such an indelible impression that to this day, lake lovers who own summer homes in the Whiteshell area still talk about the Falcon Lake UFO; no doubt that discussion was a lot louder and more exaggerated in the era of flower power and free love. And so the police were obliged to investigate, regardless of their personal take on the situation. Besides, there was something about Michalak, something sincere and compelling that, despite his apparent inconsistencies and obvious deceptions, kept the interest of the authorities.

Davis and Zacharias continued to touch base with Michalak daily following their initial interviews of May 23 and 24. The officers were still hoping Michalak would recover from his ordeal and feel well enough to accompany them to locate the alleged landing site of the foreign aircraft. But by May 30, they temporarily satisfied their quest for his input by asking Michalak to draw a map of the area where he believed his sighting occurred. Davis and a team of investigators made their way back to Falcon Lake. They were anxious to locate the event site because they believed any trace of the aircraft, if indeed there had been an aircraft, would be increasingly difficult to find as the days and weeks wore on and the lush vegetation of spring crept over the previously barren landscape.

Davis and his colleague Constable Anderson met Squadron Leader Bissky at Falcon Lake. From there the investigators once again boarded a helicopter, on loan from the Canadian Army and piloted by Captain Bruce Muelander, and toured the area Michalak had sketched out for them. According to Michalak's description, they were looking for "a flat piece of rock approximately 300 feet [90 metres] long by 100 feet [30 metres] wide." As Davis explained in his report of the trip, "such outcroppings of rock that size are very rare in the Falcon Lake area." The site should have been easy to identify if Michalak's map of the area was accurate. But the team could not spot the site by helicopter, and when they took to the woods on foot, they were no more successful. After a day of fruitless efforts, investigators called off the search.

There was no two ways about it—they needed Michalak's direct input if they were ever going to find the location of his sighting. Davis and Anderson decided to return to Winnipeg and do everything they could to convince Michalak to make the outing.

The following day, Michalak agreed to make the trip to Falcon Lake. He was still feeling the effects of his experiences and complained that he was unwell, but he promised to do his best to find the spot where he'd allegedly seen the aircraft. Again, their efforts fell flat, although as Davis pointed out in his report, Michalak was convinced the ground search portion of the investigation "had been very, very close to the sought-after location as he recognized several physical features and areas where he had chipped rocks during his last prospecting visit."

During the search, Michalak seemed confused and agitated. To Davis, it looked as though he was grasping at straws:

...we walked for most of the afternoon covering some-where between 3 and 4 miles [5 and 6.5 kilometres] of dense bush and outcroppings of rock without finding anything of value. Michalak seemed to be wandering aimlessly through the bush and didn't really appear to know where he was going. His excuse for acting like this was that he claimed when he was prospecting he followed quartz veins in the rock facings and didn't really pay any attention to where he was going. He says

he would walk for most of the day and then when he felt he had gone far enough to leave himself enough time to get out before dark he would take a compass reading and head out to whichever direction he thought the highway was...

Michalak's disorientation frustrated investigators, but ufologists such as Chris Rutkowski, who have closely monitored these kinds of accounts for decades, didn't discredit Michalak because of his apparent confusion. It made sense, Rutkowski reasoned. Who wouldn't be disoriented after going through what Michalak had experienced? Countless stories of people enduring any kind of trauma report similar behaviours to those that Michalak exhibited. In any case, the situation was disappointing. Once again investigators returned home without the answers they were looking for, and the location of the landing site would remain a mystery for some time to come.

Although the landing site had yet to be identified, and investigators continued to search the wilderness surrounding Falcon Beach, an official from the "UFO Project for the United States Government at the University of Colorado, Boulder, Colorado," had arrived in Winnipeg. According to an RCMP report dated June 26, the university had received a grant from the American government to finance a year-long research project on the topic of unidentified flying objects. Dr. Roy Craig, who was heading this project, had taken it upon himself to travel to Winnipeg and interview Michalak on June 3, to assess the situation for himself. Craig was reportedly impressed with

Michalak's story, but like the Canadian officials involved in the case, Craig was dismayed at the man's confusion when the two eventually travelled to Falcon Lake.

With Michalak back at home and still recovering from his ordeal, investigators continued to make repeated trips between Winnipeg and Falcon Lake, hoping to stumble upon something that amounted to physical evidence. On June 8, Squadron Leader Bissky returned to the lake with another angle to check out. This time he and his colleagues were going to look at the microwave tower located near the area they thought Michalak might have been exploring. They were working with the theory that Michalak may have climbed the tower to gain a better visual perspective of the area and gage what might be the most promising locations to look for his cherished quartz veins. Was it possible, investigators pondered, that Michalak somehow burned himself on that microwave tower? This theory fell by the wayside after Bissky assessed the situation himself and decided it was highly unlikely that theory could hold water. But he didn't come away from his efforts totally empty-handed. By climbing the tower, he noticed a spot that looked like what Michalak had been trying to explain in his sketch.

Bissky descended the tower and was once again hoofing it through the bush, hoping to find some of the items Michalak said he'd left behind on his travels— the garbage bag and the saw, or the steel tape Michalak had since realized was missing and might have been left behind in his haste to get back to Falcon Beach campground. And again, Bissky's efforts didn't bear fruit. It was the last straw as far as the RCAF was concerned. The squadron leader informed Davis that the matter was "closed pending Michalak locating the spot and supplying further information."

Although Dr. Craig was a credible investigator in the eyes of the RCMP and RCAF, Davis had some concerns about Mr. Thompson and APRO. Before following through with his superiors' suggestion to contact Thompson and try to collaborate with APRO, Davis checked out the organization. Dr. Craig told Davis that APRO had a reputation for looking for stories of UFO sightings to sell to magazines and other news agencies. It also looked like there wasn't a lot of communication between members of the organization.

According to Craig, Thompson might not be the only APRO man in a city the size of Winnipeg, and it was possible Thompson wouldn't be aware of any of the others. Davis felt his concerns about collaborating with APRO were justified; Bissky and many of Davis' other colleagues agreed. At this point, the investigation would maintain its local focus; officers would not collaborate with Thompson. And while the investigation remained a priority for Davis and his colleagues, the daily routine outside of the Falcon Lake Incident was beginning to settle back in to a regular pace.

Life was starting to revert back to normal for Michalak, as well—as far as his work life was concerned. On June 5, after spending two weeks at home, the mechanic was finally back on the job. He was reportedly regaining some of the weight he'd lost, as well as much of his strength, and many of his other symptoms had subsided. Requests for interviews with the man had decreased, perhaps giving Michalak a chance to digest his experience. Still, investigators had kept the lines of communication open and told Michalak that they were still interested in exploring the region if he located the landing site.

As the weeks passed, it became increasingly clear that finding the location of Michalak's alleged encounter would be a large factor in substantiating his story. The test results were coming back on the samples Michalak had provided from his experience—samples he picked up when he eventually returned to the site without alerting the officials of his actions and that were sent off to various labs for analysis—and the report seemed to support some of Michalak's claims. According to Staff Sergeant L.H. Winters, "earth samples from [the] scene [were] highly radioactive." Furthermore, the "soil sample, steel tape and burned clothing obtained from [the] Defence Research Board Lab [in] Ottawa" had tested positive for radiation.

On July 24, 1967, the Physics Section of the RCMP Crime Detection Laboratory in Ottawa also submitted a report, this time regarding the three items Michalak provided for testing the previous month. While the samples registered high levels of radioactivity, officials were disturbed that the supporting information on the case was, as they put it, "vague and disjointed." It stymied investigators that despite his earlier interest in working with the RCMP and RCAF, Michalak was now refusing to cooperate. In fact, they had declared Michalak was in general uncooperative "toward the military and police."

The problem was that no one had a clue why Michalak had changed loyalties.

After a little probing, officials tied this sudden change in Michalak's behaviour to the appearance of a new person on the scene, a man by the name of Gerald Hart.

Hart contacted Michalak on the weekend of June 24. According to the information Michalak provided investigators, he had never met Hart prior to that time. And while the reports are altogether unclear about how a complete stranger would have provoked such unconditional trust in the otherwise leery and secretive Michalak, the fact remained that Hart had managed to do just that. The new affiliation between the two men caused investigators considerable concern. A later report penned by noted Winnipeg ufologist Chris Rutkowski in October 1999 stated the RCAF viewed Hart as a "subversive," and that he was known to the authorities as an individual with radical opinions: they pointed to his stance on how to avoid paying income tax, the topic of a book he wrote, as just one example of his subversive nature.

In his report, Davis reviewed the inconsistencies in Michalak's actions:

From the outset of this investigation he [Michalak] *pointed out to us that he was concerned about too many people knowing where his claims were and he wanted to confine the knowledge to the RCMP and RCAF members who were working on the case. At no time did he indicate any unwillingness to take our members and Sqdn/Ldr Bissky to the scene and in fact on a number of occasions he told us how anxious he was to do so...*

As far as Davis was concerned, it was Hart's presence on the case that had changed Michalak's behaviour. Through his finely tuned powers of persuasion, Hart had convinced Michalak to consider a partnership with him.

Davis learned of Michalak's association with Hart after Bissky and Constable Anderson visited the prospector on June 26. Unable to make the visit himself because of another commitment, Davis had asked Anderson to interview Michalak again, this time with Bissky. Michalak was shaken when he saw the officials standing at his door; he believed they were there to interrogate him about his return to the site of his encounter and wondered how the officers could have known about it. In his report, Davis wasn't clear if the investigators indeed knew of Michalak's visit prior to their arrival or if their unannounced appearance the

day after the man's trip to the lake was only a coincidence. Either way, their arrival on Michalak's doorstep
was disconcerting to the prospector, and it took him
some time to gather himself together and discuss what,
if anything, he and Hart had discovered.

It was during this visit that Michalak produced the
"evidence" he'd retrieved from the scene, but he agreed
to show the items only to Bissky:

> …[Michalak] *said prior to going downstairs that he*
> *had some rocks that he had brought back from there*
> *that he wanted to show to Sqdn/Ldr Bissky. He then*
> *brought out a plastic bag containing some dirt and*
> *what appeared to be pieces of a green shirt or at least*
> *material that had been burned. He also had a steel*
> *tape that he said he had brought from the scene and*
> *some burned moss. He handed over a small sample of*
> *this material, dirt and the tape, to Sqdn/Ldr Bissky*
> *for forwarding to Ottawa…*

Bissky reported that Michalak, with Hart backing
his decision, told the officer that under no conditions
was he interested in taking officials to the landing
site "until he had filed his mineral claim and the
analyst's reply came back from Ottawa on the rock
samples he had brought back from the scene." The
change in Michalak's attitude was frustrating, and
the second reason the prospector gave for his sudden
change of heart only confused Davis further. Anderson
reported that Michalak said he was angry about the
"character, personal history and background enquiries"
Davis had conducted on him following the initial

interviews. This didn't make any sense at all to Davis: before he'd contacted any of the individuals in question he'd explained to Michalak that it was common practice to follow through with these additional interviews, and Michalak knew he had, for the most part, received only positive comments.

Although the reasons for Michalak's seemingly erratic behaviour had been conveniently explained away, it didn't change how Davis felt about the situation. Furthermore, Michalak had gone against a direct request by Davis to let the officers know if he was making a trip to the lake, and to refrain from removing any evidence from the scene if he managed to find the site. Michalak denied hearing either of these requests from Davis.

That Michalak provided test samples to Bissky during the late-June meeting, along with photographs the two men had taken that "showed indications of [a] burned circle" measuring 4.5 metres (14.5 feet) in diameter, was only a small consolation to investigators. Michalak was being continuously evasive. Even a month later, on July 26, when Bissky, Davis, a Mr. D. Thompson of the Manitoba Health Department and a Mr. Stuart E. Hunt, a radiation expert with the Radiation Protection Division of the Department of Health and Welfare, yet again asked Michalak to accompany them to the site, he still refused to do so, stating he would "lose too much money by missing a day's work."

Was it possible that Michalak and Hart were orchestrating an intricate hoax? If so, what could they possibly hope to gain? Even if Michalak was trying to sell his story for profit, whatever money he might receive had to be nominal, certainly not enough to share with Hart. Although public interest in the topic of UFOs was certainly on the rise, any notoriety on the subject couldn't possibly be worth the stress Michalak had felt over the last few months. If there never was a flying saucer, and Michalak had made up the entire story, drawing attention to the area where he believed he'd discovered a significant mineral deposit was probably not to his benefit. And if the encounter was indeed a fabrication, how did the items Michalak turned over as evidence register what many referred to as unusual levels of Radium-226?

In light of Michalak's attitude change toward members of the RCMP, Davis and his colleagues initially decided to step back and "leave any remaining enquiries and contact with Michalak to the RCAF." But then there was the small matter of a telex from the commissioner, dated July 24, that couldn't be ignored:

> *Laboratory Tests here indicate earth samples taken from scene highly radioactive. Radiation Protection Div. of Dept. of Health and Welfare concerned that others may be exposed, if travel in area not restricted. Suggest you close off area completely.... Determine whether Michalak has been examined medically from radioactive exposure aspect.*

Bissky, who was away on holidays when this information arrived, cut his vacation short as soon as Davis told him of the contents of the telex. Bissky was concerned because the soil samples registering the high levels of radiation were only a small portion of the soil Michalak had in his basement. What was left of that soil could pose a significant health hazard to the man and his family, and perhaps even the community at large. That an important official like Hunt was scheduled to arrive in Winnipeg on July 27 was another factor in Bissky's decision to return home early.

Clearly, the powers that be were concerned. Maybe there was some truth to Michalak's wild and rambling story after all. Maybe the authorities were remiss in not having dealt with the information more effectively. More than two months had passed since the initial report was filed. That meant people hiking in the area could have been exposed to dangerous levels of radiation. If, however, Michalak was orchestrating a farce, he had somehow acquired radioactive materials, which also posed a danger to the community.

Although he remained committed to keeping his distance from Michalak, and despite his earlier misgivings about the idea, Davis decided to approach Barry Thompson of APRO in a last-ditch attempt to get to the bottom of the situation. Davis learned that Michalak had taken Thompson to the landing site on July 17. Davis discovered that Thompson had been given several samples from the site, courtesy of Michalak, and that the APRO man had sent those samples to his organization's headquarters in Tucson.

Perhaps, Davis reasoned, Thompson would agree to go with officials to the landing site because Michalak still appeared reluctant to do so. Apparently pleased with the request, Thompson accompanied Hunt and Bissky to the site.

In the meantime, Davis was also preparing himself for a visit with Michalak. It would be the first time the two men would speak since Davis learned about Michalak's feelings about the investigation. Davis was still hoping Michalak would agree to go with the group to the site, and Davis was bringing Hunt, Thompson and Bissky along to the interview. Davis wanted Hunt to share first-hand the laboratory results he'd collected and to impose on Michalak the potential seriousness of the situation.

Surprisingly, Michalak agreed to Davis' request. This apparent change of heart left investigators confused, especially considering that the man denied the exact same request just the day before. According to Davis' official report, the day after his most recent interview, Michalak was "courteous and appeared completely cooperative in every respect." Davis agreed to contact Inland Cement to arrange for Michalak to have a weekday off: Davis was hoping to avoid the large weekend crowds that typically flooded the resort community that time of year, though it would be difficult to avoid them altogether since it was July, and summer holidays were in full swing.

While Davis called Michalak's boss, Hunt used his radiation-detection equipment to check radiation levels in Michalak's home. During the process, Michalak took Hunt to the soil samples he still had in his basement. Although the rest of the house was not contaminated, the soil samples registered positive for radiation. With a few of the remaining samples in hand, Hunt and Michalak returned to Davis and the rest of the team. On learning that the plans for a return trip to Falcon Lake had been confirmed for the following day, Davis and his colleagues bid Michalak good night.

Michalak seemed agreeable during his most recent interaction with members of the initial investigative team, but he may have felt quite differently had he known of the trip Hunt and his colleague D. Thompson had made the day before. There was some conjecture among investigators that Michalak could have intentionally caused the radioactive readings on the samples he provided to convince the authorities of his encounter. Michalak could have done this in two ways, investigators speculated. One theory was that he could have "seeded the landing site with commercially produced radium...from a radium watch dial." The second theory was even more interesting; he could have collected contaminated samples from a nuclear waste disposal site. The average Manitoban might not have known this at the time, and most probably don't know about it now, but as luck would have it, there was just such a site not more than a stone's throw from the resort community of Falcon Lake near the community of East Braintree.

On the morning of July 27, prior to the meeting with Michalak, Hunt and Thompson travelled to East Braintree and met with a Mr. R. Kemp, conservation officer for the Renewable Resources Branch of Manitoba's Department of Mines and Natural Resources. The investigative team learned that the Manitoba Cancer Clinic had used a plot of land near the small community located along Highway 1, just west of Falcon Lake, as a disposal site. Thanks to a Mr. E. Campbell, an official from the clinic who had provided investigators with photographs of the area for reference, Hunt and Thompson found the site without any difficulty despite the fact that it was overgrown and nearly unrecognizable otherwise.

> *Only one of the steel spikes used to mark the burial site could be located…. It appeared to us that the soils had not been disturbed as most of the area was covered with vegetation. Another two years will see the area completely overgrown with vegetation. No radiation checks were made as there was a minimum of 3 feet [90 centimetres] of sand covering the contaminated materials. The maximum amount of radium located at the burial site is in the area of 12 mgms.*

At this point, timelines differ between the official report Hunt eventually submitted to the Safety Assessment and Control Section of the Radiation Protection Division and the one Davis submitted to his superiors. It seems that Hunt might have erred in the dates he applied to the events of July 28 as having taken place on July 27, but the information about what occurred when Michalak accompanied the entourage of officials to what he believed was the landing site was the same.

Both reports agreed that the landing site was identified within a short time—it only took about 45 minutes according to Hunt. Constable Zacharias, who had previously travelled to the location with APRO's Barry Thompson, confirmed the location. The area also closely resembled the map Michalak had outlined for investigators and wasn't too far from their first attempt to pinpoint it—only about "40 or 50 yards [12 or 15 metres] from a large rock where Constable Anderson, Michalak and I had been during the unsuccessful search on June 1," Davis wrote in his report. Davis went on to state that Michalak "said that he felt the main reason he could not find the right place during his previous attempts was because too many people were involved and were suggesting various places for him to look at." As it turned out, Michalak may have been disoriented, but he was not too far off the mark.

There were, however, several notable differences between Michalak's sketch and description and the actual landing site as identified on July 28. Davis observed that it was "considerably smaller and not as open as we had been given to believe." It also didn't have the wide-open area Michalak spoke so fervently about. In fact, it was the lack of an open space that deterred officials from investigating that area further during their earlier visit.

Regardless of the discrepancies, the significant levels of radiation in Michalak's samples meant that, with an eye on public safety, the authorities had to leave nothing to chance and investigate the area thoroughly. Davis described the "landing site" as:

> ... [a] *semi-circle on the rock face measuring approximately 15 ft.* [4.5 metres] *in diameter where the moss had been somehow removed. About the southern one third of the outline is missing due to a depression in the rock at that point but the remainder of the circle can be clearly seen. Michalak pointed to a spot void of some moss near the circle where he claims he stood when he touched the UFO and where he dropped his burning outer shirt...*

Davis went on to explain that Michalak then pointed out the rock on which he'd been chipping away at a vein of quartz; it was about 200 feet (60 metres) due south of the alleged landing spot. Because the area didn't mirror Michalak's earlier description, the officer then took a compass reading of the site. It recorded 020-degrees, "...a sharp conflict from [Michalak's] earlier statements where he said he took a compass reading after the vehicle left and it was exactly 255-degrees south southwest..."

Meanwhile, Hunt was busy checking for radiation levels. Using several pieces of portable survey equipment used to measure radioactivity—a Tracerlab SU14, Admiral Radiac 5016, and a Civil Defence CDV 700, which were all different types—traces of radiation were indeed picked up. But the levels were low, and all of the positive readings were located near the "fault in the rock across the centre of the landing spot." Altogether, Hunt estimated the contaminated area was "no larger than 100 square inches [645 square centimetres]."

Nearby water sources were negative for radiation contamination, as was any of the surrounding vegetation. Because the area in question was so small, most of the contaminated materials were being removed, and the location was so remote, officials at the site decided there was "no serious health hazard involved" and that further precautions were unnecessary.

Some of the samples removed from the site were immediately checked under an ultraviolet light source. The results suggested they might have been contaminated with a radium luminous compound commonly found, at the time, in paint products used in "watch and clock faces, maritime compasses, and a variety of military items and aircraft instruments."

According to the Canadian Nuclear Safety Commission, a radium luminous compound, also known as Radium-226 or Ra-226 in the scientific community, "consists of radium salts mixed with a chemical phosphor." The combination produces a luminescence— a great additive for producing glow-in-the-dark paint, which is extremely useful if you want to tell the time in the dark. The compound is dangerous to human health if it is "ingested, inhaled or absorbed through the skin." Although using it to highlight watch faces and instrument panels meant the actual compound was usually behind glass, there was enough of a risk to public health and safety that the Canadian government banned the production of radium luminous products by 1970.

The samples were sent to various laboratories for further analysis. But there was a lot of legwork investigators could do while they waited for the results.

The first order of business investigators had in mind was to make inquiries at the Inland Cement Company to see if Ra-226, or any other radium source, was used. Hunt and his colleagues visited Inland Cement on August 1, and their queries on the matter included both the Regina and the Winnipeg locations because Michalak had worked in both places. Management confirmed that Ra-226 was not used at either plant.

The following day, members of the research team visited Thompson at his home in Oakdean Gardens. They wanted to check out the samples Michalak had given Thompson, but on arriving at his residence, they learned those samples had been placed at his mother's home in St. Vital. Concerned about the possibility of excessive radiation levels, the team convinced Thompson to accompany them to his mother's residence. Once there, the team checked the rock and vegetation sample, which registered negative for radiation. The same was not true, however, for the soil sample.

In his report, Hunt stated that, "Levels up to 1 MR/hr were detected." (According to the World Nuclear Association, the "global average of naturally occurring background radiation" ranges between 0.17 and 0.39 microseverts per hour.) Worried about Thompson and his family's safety, investigators scanned the entire home for further contamination using an ultraviolet light. According to Hunt's report, a few areas responded to the UV light. On closer examination, it was determined that this wasn't because of any contamination but was more likely a result of "photographic emulsion splashes."

The visit with Thompson also gave Hunt and his colleagues a more in-depth understanding of APRO, their sphere of influence in the world of ufology and their presence in Winnipeg. The investigators confirmed that Thompson was aware of other APRO associates living in the city and that at the time there were about 15 members in the Winnipeg chapter of the organization. Of that number, only four were "investigating members." It appears as though the only criterion to become a member was that the individual had to be 21 years or older, and the majority of the group was considerably younger than Thompson, which may have reduced the group's credibility in the eyes of the investigators.

Thompson either did not know or chose not to share the identity of other APRO members. And although Thompson told investigators that he'd passed some of the samples he'd collected from Michalak on to the Nuclear Medicine Department of what was then known as the Winnipeg General Hospital, he withheld the name of the technician who'd agreed to conduct a "spectral analysis" without, according to Thompson, prior approval from his superiors. He went on to say that two of the three samples submitted recorded "very weak energy peaks," but one soil sample registered a "1.4 mev [mega-electron volt] peak." At the time, Thompson denied knowing where those samples ended up.

Not willing to let the ball drop just yet, investigators visited the Winnipeg General Hospital on August 3 and identified the technician Thompson spoke with as George Dyck. Contrary to Thompson's suggestion, Dyck said his supervisors were aware of the samples being checked and at least a cursory reason for the request. Dyck explained that the analysts had even decided to go a step further and conduct a second analysis in the hope of deriving more specific information.

Dyck then introduced Hunt and the team to Dr. F. Helmuth. Helmuth told investigators that sometime following Michalak's initial encounter he'd examined the man and thought his burns might have been of a thermal nature. With that in mind, he sent Michalak to Pinawa Hospital—with a nuclear plant in the immediate area, the hospital specialized in radiation treatment. In Pinawa, Dr. Petco examined Michalak and placed him in the "W.B.C." (the whole body count room, as it was called, was a soundproof isolation room where patients who were thought to have been exposed to radiation would be tested for the levels in their body).

In Petco's professional opinion, Michalak would benefit from psychiatric treatment; Helmuth didn't think that was necessary. Either way, Helmuth explained that the initial and follow-up analysis of the samples Thompson provided were conducted before the doctor had a clear understanding of the entire situation. Helmuth, along with Dr. R.J. Walton of the Manitoba Cancer Clinic, agreed to return the samples to Hunt, who would then forward them to Ottawa.

Meanwhile, concerns about radiation levels and any possible health side effects from exposure to that radiation were on the rise among some of the individuals who were aware of Michalak's encounter, and who'd been following the investigation. Gerald Hart had contacted Bissky asking if his car and place of business could be checked for contamination. After accompanying Michalak back to Falcon Lake earlier that summer, and returning to the city with samples from the alleged landing site, Hart was concerned for his own personal health and safety.

Investigators met with Hart on August 2 but didn't discover any traces of contamination at Hart Electronics or in his car. At the same time, that newest encounter with Hart proved to be somewhat revelatory. In his report, Hunt explained that Hart seemed "very interested in 'Inters[t]ellar Vehicles'" and had apparently witnessed several in his lifetime. "He even shot at one while duck hunting near Beausejour," Hunt reported.

If that wasn't strange enough, Hart also admitted that he was "in the process of developing a device which can be used for detecting 'Interstellar Vehicles.'" When asked to see the instrument he was working on, Hart told investigators that he'd loaned the circuitry to a friend, though he didn't elaborate on what that friend was planning to do with it.

Between Thompson and APRO, and Hart and his personal endeavours, it was increasingly clear to investigators that the perceived threat from otherworldly sources was weighing heavily on a particular segment of the general population. With that in mind, coming to a conclusion about Michalak and his experiences of May 20 was even more desirable.

Unfortunately for all concerned, including Michalak, it wasn't looking like any conclusion to this case was even a remote possibility.

By the end of the summer of 1967, the investigation surrounding Michalak and his strange experience that afternoon in May was, like the lingering summer sun, little more than a memory, at least when it came to Canadian officials. Files into the investigation were now closed.

Hunt's report to Ottawa acknowledged "radioactive contamination of rock and lichens" at the Falcon Lake site Michalak identified. At one point there was some speculation that perhaps the remote area had been used some time in the not-too-distant past as a dumpsite for radioactive materials discarded from the Manitoba Cancer Clinic, but no evidence was ever uncovered to support that theory. At the end of Hunt's investigation, the origin of the contamination in the rock and soil samples was not identified.

Davis' report to his superiors at RCMP headquarters was equally inconclusive. The discrepancies in Michalak's story remained a stumbling block to investigators. In particular, the conflicting information of Michalak claiming he hadn't consumed alcohol the night before his encounter, and the Falcon Lake bartender's comments about serving the man five bottles of beer, still didn't sit well with officials. Michalak's disorientation and aimless wanderings during the first attempt to visit the alleged landing site, and the discrepancy between what Michalak claimed were his compass readings and those recorded by the officers when they finally managed to see the site, also raised red flags for investigators.

The fact that Michalak contacted Hart after specifically telling officers he didn't want anyone to know the location of the site in order to protect his claim didn't win the man any brownie points either. And finally,

Michalak's decision to remove evidence from the scene after being explicitly ordered not to was outright defiant—and led investigators to speculate that the so-called evidence had been tampered with. Whichever way they looked at it, in their eyes, Michalak wasn't a completely credible witness.

At the same time, the RCMP report couldn't flatly deny Michalak's alleged incident without experiencing a whole lot of cognitive dissonance. In the end, they concluded that, although they couldn't prove what it may have been, it was clear something untoward happened to the man while prospecting the Manitoba wilderness that Saturday afternoon in May. There were simply too many factors that supported Michalak's story:

> *...there are certain facts that cannot be denied and cannot be accounted for or explained away. These include* [Michalak's] *illness, headache, and loss of weight during a two-week period immediately after the alleged sighting; a fluctuation in his blood cell count that occurred at the same time; the burns to his chest, abdomen and clothing as well as the circle on the rock where he alleges the UFO landed. Our investigation has not been able to resolve any of those points mentioned and we have not been able to account for the inconsistent actions of Michalak..."*

Regardless of the number of unanswered questions that remained, the case of the Falcon Lake Incident from both the perspective of the RCMP and the Department of National Defence was closed.

For Michalak, the ramifications of the case never ended. He couldn't accept that he'd live the rest of his life not knowing what really happened that afternoon at Falcon Lake. In a way, if it wasn't for the geese and their noisy response to the craft Michalak saw, he would have gone to his grave thinking he'd hallucinated the entire thing. The geese were there, and if they could talk, they would have supported his story. But they couldn't talk, and Michalak spent the rest of his life dealing with the consequences of an encounter he would replay until the day he died at the age of 83. At some point he would even travel to the Mayo Clinic in Rochester, Minnesota, as an outpatient, hoping for some answers about the residual effects of that now-infamous prospecting trip, but even the Mayo Clinic couldn't give him any insight into the physical side effects that would trouble him to the end of his life.

Chris Rutkowski, the Winnipeg author and ufologist, and coincidentally a childhood friend of one of Michalak's sons, spoke affectionately about the well-known and well-loved gentleman in an obituary he penned on October 30, 1999. He remembered how Michalak "stubbornly refused to give in to pressure, and boldly and tirelessly told visitors and callers about his experience." Rutkowski points out that Michalak's story never varied—the details were always the same. And strangely enough, Michalak never thought that what he'd seen was anything otherworldly at all; he simply believed he saw a modern, potentially top secret, foreign aircraft.

The story that is perhaps most telling about Michalak's personality is an interaction Rutkowski witnessed between the man and a film crew from the television series *Unsolved Mysteries*:

> *Just before rolling film, the director wanted Michalak to relax and feel more comfortable in front of the cameras. He began talking with him about the weather, his work, what Canada was like and other nonchalant topics. Then, the director said, "Well, Steve, I guess your being burned by the UFO was the most incredible thing that has ever happened in your life." To the surprise of everyone on the set, Michalak answered, "Oh, no it wasn't." Prodded further, Michalak bravely told the story of his experiences in the Nazi death camps...*

Rutkowski's testimony about Michalak's character during the course of his life remains in stark contrast with the kind of man who would contrive a false story about a strange encounter—a story that could potentially stir fear in the hearts of area residents. Something strange happened, Michalak was certain, and everyone deserved an explanation.

Sadly, an explanation would not come—at least not during Michalak's lifetime.

MacGregor: In the Dark of Night

...We both know about the rumours (concerning a captured UFO and crew members at the Wright-Patterson Air Force Base in Dayton, Ohio). I have never seen what I would call a UFO, but I have intelligent friends who have.

–U.S. Senator, U.S. Air Force General and
one-time presidential candidate,
Barry Goldwater, April 11, 1979

Eighteen-year-old Gerald Adams had a lot on his mind on the evening of October 24, 1970. He had a girlfriend he'd been enamoured with for some time, and he had planned an exciting date that Saturday. After a busy and eventful night, as he drove the young lady of his heart home, he must have thought there was no better way to end the evening than to do a little stargazing.

It was a beautiful night—perhaps one of the last such nights that part of the country would see until spring; the snow is often knee deep by Halloween. Manitoba winters can be ruthless, especially in the wide-open prairie land that surrounds much of the stretch of Highway 1 between Winnipeg and Brandon. Without many trees to offer cover, winter winds are sharp and cutting, and the damp air can feel like it's seeping right through your body and into your bones. But on this night the temperature was hovering around the freezing mark. Skies were clear.

You could see the northern lights. And if you were patient, the night was offering up its own rendition of fireworks with a display of shooting stars.

A lovely night like this was just too marvellous to pass up.

Gerald nudged and prodded his girlfriend until she eventually relented to go for a drive, and the couple meandered down the back roads just outside of the small, prairie town of MacGregor, Manitoba. When they found what Gerald thought was a suitable location, where the lovebirds weren't likely to be disturbed, he parked his truck, "facing north on a trail road about 3 or 4 miles [5 or 6.5 kilometres] north of town."

It was about 1:00 AM when the two young lovers got comfortable, snuggling close enough to whisper endearments to one another. Suddenly, a bright light appeared out of nowhere. It surely startled the two teens—farm folk typically turn in long before this time of night, and most of the fields had been cultivated so the chance that a farmer was out and about was highly unlikely. The couple sat up to see what was going on. "We noticed a bright light. We thought it was a car coming," Gerald said in a letter to Peter Millman of the National Research Council of Canada.

What the two lovebirds saw was anything but a car.

Peering through the truck windows, Gerald and his lady saw what looked like an oblong-shaped object measuring about 1 or 1.5 metres in height, and about 2.5 metres in diameter, glowing in the field about 800 metres northwest of their location. Nine poles crowned with red lights protruded from the top of the object in groups of three. Something that looked like a dark-coloured flange seemed to wrap around the craft about 30 centimetres away from the main body, as if it was suspended in air. Above the flange Gerald thought he could make out the shape of a small window, and a "bright yellow light" spilled out into the night. When asked, Gerald later described the main body of the vessel as being a "light orangey colour."

Overhead, the shooting stars continued to light up the night sky, but their gentle falling did nothing to calm the young woman's unease. Shaken by what she saw, and unable to identify what it actually was, Gerald's girlfriend asked him his thoughts on the matter. "I told her it might be a UFO," Gerald said. "This made her a little nervous."

She was even more unsettled when Gerald suggested he walk over to the object. She was clearly uncomfortable with being left alone in the truck, and equally disturbed by the idea of accompanying Gerald in his desire to get a closer look. For a while the two just sat there and watched until finally Gerald yielded to his girlfriend's requests and drove her home.

But that wasn't the last Gerald saw of his UFO.

After a quick kiss goodnight, the young man rushed back to the spot where he'd last seen the glowing object and found that it appeared to have moved "a couple of miles away and it was hovering a little above the ground." The moon was still shining, and the sky was alight with northern lights and a plethora of stars, providing Gerald with a good view of the strange aircraft—and perhaps a peek at its inhabitants.

If Gerald had been hesitant to tell the authorities about his sighting, what he'd just witnessed was all the encouragement he needed to file a formal report.

Scant details about the experience Gerald and his girlfriend had on the night of October 24, 1970, were included in the initial UFO Report filed by a Captain G.M. Winterburn at the Canadian Forces Operations Centre. According to the report, Gerald described the strange object as somewhat "button shaped in a tapered bowl fashion." He said he thought the flange he described around the vessel's centre looked like it was spinning in a "wavering motion."

As if the vessel wasn't strange enough, Gerald then went on to describe a two-legged creature he was sure he'd seen after he returned from dropping off his girlfriend. According to the official report, Gerald saw:

One humanoid sighted approx. one half mile [800 metres] *from UFO walking with "difficult"*

*heading north. Humanoid 4 ft. [1 metre] high with
arms and legs and head in a silver metallic uniform,
appeared to be wearing a helmet. Observer at one point
within 50 ft. [15 metres] or less from humanoid.
Takes off from second location described as slowly lifting
off surface in vertical motion, then rapidly departing in
a NW direction with great speed and out of sight within
30 seconds.*

Little silver men aside, the sighting sparked enough
of an interest for Winterburn to pass the information
on to Peter M. Millman, head of the Upper Atmosphere
Research section of the National Research Council of
Canada. But the report wasn't as thorough as Millman
would have liked, so he corresponded back and forth
with Gerald for some time, asking for clarification
and suggesting explanations for what the young man
might have seen.

In particular, Millman wanted to know how Gerald
had been able to get such a good view of the craft
that night, and how the teen knew the distance
between his truck and the UFO. Millman also asked
Gerald how he managed to find the object the second
time and details about the atmospheric and weather
conditions that night.

Gerald's prompt and detailed response to the questions in Millman's letter cleared up several of the
researcher's questions. At the same time they raised
an additional concern, in particular, Gerald's claim
that there was a full moon out during his encounter.
According to Millman's calculations, the moon would

not have "risen on the night of October 24/25 until over one hour after the 1:00 AM [Gerald] listed for the original sighting." In a second letter to Gerald, Millman asked if perhaps the young man was mistaken, and if what he'd witnessed actually occurred on another day? Millman also posed a second scenario: was it possible Gerald had confused his times?

In his reply, Gerald was adamant that he had made no error on the date or time.

If questioning the date and time stirred Gerald's ire just a bit, Millman's efforts to explain Gerald's sighting certainly must have added fuel to the fire. Millman said it was possible that because the sighting of the object was, in his calculations, "almost exactly the direction of Neepawa," what Gerald saw was lights from that community. "Neepawa has at least two high towers lit with red obstruction warning lights for aircraft, and there may be other high warning lights in town," Millman explained, adding that the reflection of these images could have appeared as a "rare type of looming mirage." "The town of Neepawa would appear quite similar to what you described as seen from your location," Millman wrote to Gerald. "As the mirage condition disintegrated the appearance would correspond to what you described after you returned later, and eventually it would disappear."

Millman didn't have the same kind of elaborate explanation for what Gerald called the "small silver man." All he said was that the sighting quite likely didn't have anything to do with the larger, spaceship-like object Gerald had witnessed.

The suggestion of seeing a mirage reflected from Neepawa must have sounded outlandish to Gerald. Clearly Millman didn't understand Manitoba's geography or topography. For one thing, MacGregor is about 56 kilometres southeast of Neepawa as the crow flies—a little longer when you travel the highway. The highway is fairly curvy, with the odd hill and valley thrown in for good measure, moving the traveller along like a gentle rollercoaster. Westbourne, Gladstone and a few smaller hamlets separate the two larger communities. And though the land around MacGregor, and for a short stretch north of the Trans-Canada Highway, is typical flat farmland, that is not the case the farther north you travel. By the time one reaches Westbourne, the winding road is lined with thickets verging on forest.

To put it plainly, there's a lot that separates the two communities.

How anyone could consider that a mirage had miraculously floated along like a Star Trek holograph from Neepawa, dropping into a field near MacGregor, was dumfounding. But Millman was persistent:

Your comment of the frequency of meteors or shooting stars that night is interesting since this was close to the maximum of the Orionid meteor shower. Bright meteors from this shower would travel in general from a southeast to northwest direction, and it is possible that a very bright fireball produced the intense light which first called your attention to the phenomenon, and you may have assumed that the mirage was the landed object.

Of course, this was only a theory—and Millman stressed it wasn't "necessarily the correct explanation" for what Gerald and his girlfriend saw that night. But it's hard to discern by the tone of the letter if Millman was trying to offer Gerald a little reassurance with his words or if he was merely scoffing at the young man's suggestion, proposing that just about anything was more likely than Gerald's posit that he'd seen a UFO.

Whatever Millman's motive, Gerald didn't mince words in his quick reply. He flatly denounced Millman's conjecture and then went on to reinforce his own points. He had not seen "light on a tower" but a UFO. He was not mistaken about the date or time of his sighting, and the moon had been definitely shining when he and his girlfriend first saw the still-unidentified object. As for the small silver man, well, Gerald knew what he saw—but he didn't bother arguing that point with Millman.

With that, Gerald Adams thanked Millman and bid him a quick farewell. The only other correspondence between the two men on file at Library and Archives Canada was Millman's recognition of the receipt of Gerald's final letter.

And that appears to be where this investigation stalled.

Any mention of the MacGregor sighting that might have appeared in the area papers referred loosely to "two witnesses" who were "driving between farms" when they noticed something out of the ordinary. At least that's the way it was portrayed in one Sun Media story dated July 26, 2010. Neither Gerald Adams' name nor that of his female companion was published. The real reason the young couple were at "the right place at the right time" to witness this sighting was also glossed over.

But it's certainly not a story folks in the area are unfamiliar with, and according to at least one source, the MacGregor sighting is one of the "all-time significant UFO cases from Manitoba."

But many more strange stories have emerged from Manitoba's stark prairie and wooded lake lands. The province is a bit of a hotbed when it comes to UFO sightings. And like the MacGregor encounter, a lot of these sightings have never been identified.

Carman: Charlie Redstar

We all know that UFOs are real. All we need to ask is where do they come from.

–astronaut Edgar D. Mitchell, following his
1971 *Apollo 14* moon flight

The folks of "Friendly Manitoba" are warm and welcoming, inclined to open their doors to a stranger or give their last dollar to someone in need. At the same time, they're no-nonsense kind of folks who don't mind getting their hands dirty with hard work.

This is especially true of the province's rural residents. Farmers are the backbone of Manitoba's economy: agriculture has been one of the province's most important industries as well as a main source of income and employment since the first large-scale farm was founded in the Selkirk area in 1812. Farming is a hard way of life—a lifestyle that's at the mercy of Mother Nature, which can wipe out a promising crop with torrential rains or golf-ball-sized hail, a sudden summer freeze or a frenzied tornado. There's no time to entertain wild imaginings when there's always so much work to do.

So when a flurry of sightings was reported to various RCMP detachments in and around the south-central community of Carman, and from several different witnesses, the authorities took notice.

Stephenfield resident Irene Bourgeois was rocked out of a sound sleep at 2:05 AM on April 10, 1975. Some unknown object appeared to zoom over her house, and by the sounds of it, the aircraft was flying low, maybe less than 15 metres overhead. It was the loud roar and "high-pitched whizzing sound" that startled the sleeping woman.

Seconds later, her daughter, Sharon, pounded on Bourgeois' bedroom door. Sharon had fallen asleep on the couch and was wakened by a loud noise, and she was shocked to see the living room flooded by a bright red light. She wanted her mother to see the strange light, which now hovered over the tops of the trees about a kilometre south of their home.

Irene grabbed her binoculars to get a better look. What she described as "reddish orange and bluish green lights" seemed to dance across the treetops, neither growing nor shrinking in size. When asked, Bourgeois couldn't really say if the object landed or hovered. The spectacle continued until about 2:30 AM, when the lights suddenly disappeared. The entire episode was unsettling, but the fact that Irene and Sharon weren't the only ones to witness the phenomenon was somewhat comforting to them.

When Robert Diemert and his wife, Elaine, first approached Corrie Pauls of Carman on the evening of April 10 about a strange red light they'd seen, Corrie admits she wasn't overly concerned. The Diemerts asked Corrie and her husband, Frank, if they'd also seen the light. As it so happened, the couple had, but they really hadn't thought much about it. Living in a house that was situated about 137 metres northeast of the Friendship Field Airport, which the Diemerts owned, the Pauls assumed they'd seen a light from a plane.

The Diemerts weren't so readily convinced of the easy explanation, especially if what Corrie and Frank had seen was the same thing Elaine witnessed around 9:10 that night. As far as Elaine was concerned, the red light she'd seen was anything but typical. Elaine and Robert were walking down the road when they noticed the light travelling in an easterly direction. If the source of the light was a plane, they should have heard something by that point. Instead, the night air was strangely silent. In a statement transcribed by RCMP, Elaine provided her version of the story:

> *The object, which was then thought to be a UFO seemed to be the view of a wing of an aircraft while in the centre there was a brighter red, more round type of fuselage. The parts of the wing-like areas were a lighter shade of red. The colour eminating* [sic] *from the UFO seemed to be pulsating and as the object (UFO came even with our position, the UFO veered in a north to northeasterly direction.)*

The couple watched the object flying low, barely skimming the treetops, for more than five minutes. Robert was no stranger to aircraft. As an expert in restoration of vintage models, and a pilot with more than 3000 hours in the air, he knew more than most laypeople about the shapes and movements of planes.

Once the light disappeared from sight, the couple considered jumping in the car and driving north to see if they could discover it again but changed their mind, reasoning the UFO would be long gone by then anyway.

Robert's recollections echoed his wife's statement, but in more detail. Robert remarked that the night was so clear he could see Venus shining, and the couple was enjoying the starry night when his wife pointed out the strange lights. They discussed various possibilities of what the light might be and pondered the idea that because it was moving so slowly, it might be a helicopter from Portage la Prairie, a small city to the northwest of Carman.

But the closer the object approached, the more noticeable its lights became, and Robert was convinced it wasn't any kind of aircraft he'd ever seen. If it was an aircraft, it looked to Robert that the "entire wing-leading edge" was lit in red. And as it passed the couple, Robert was more convinced than ever that what they were witnessing was a UFO. Rather than darting fast and hard, this UFO seemed to drift slightly in one direction and then another, as if it wasn't sure what it wanted to do. The only light he could see was red, and he considered the thought that the red brightness he was seeing wasn't a light at all, but rather a "glow emanating from the UFO."

Constable Ian Lloyd Nicholson of the Carman Detachment took down all the witness statements, which Corporal F.B. Savage then collated and forwarded to the Upper Atmosphere Research Section of the Astrophysics Branch of the National Research Council in Ottawa. The corporal noted Robert Diemert's credentials and the weather conditions at the time of the sightings, and then he closed the file. At that point, the officers at the Carman Detachment had done all they could to further the investigation.

But what would become known as the case of Charlie Redstar was far from over.

Robert Diemert was out repairing some of the lights on his airport runway and scouting for breaks in the wire shortly before midnight of May 7, 1975, with his wife and two friends, Harold Taylor and Robert Shelton, when he witnessed the strange red light once again.

I didn't spot it immediately because I was partially blinded by the car light, but my wife Elaine said, "Oh my God, here he comes again." I immediately rushed to the car, shut off the lights, turned the motor off and by this time my night vision was beginning to return. What I saw was an elongated red light at approx. 1000 ft. [305 metres] and possibly better than 1 mile [1.5 kilometres] distant and travelling at a speed of between 80 and 100 mph [130 and 160 kilometres per hour] flying roughly parallel to the highway from Graysville to Carman. The object appeared to skirt the town.

Again, no one heard a sound, and everyone who witnessed the event was intrigued. This time Diemert and his associates climbed into the car and "gave chase." While Robert drove, the others in the car shouted directions until it disappeared, apparently heading in the direction of Winnipeg.

Once again, the witnesses filed a report with the Carman RCMP. The story so closely echoed the sighting of April 10 that it was uncanny. The most striking feature of the UFO was the intensity of its red glow. As Robert explained:

The whole thing was red, the centre brighter. No flashing lights, no green or white strobe lights. If it had been an airplane, the green light would have been facing us due to the direction of flight, but the red light was too big for a navigational light and the whole vehicle was lit up. Personally I think it was the same as I saw before, only farther away.

Diemert watched the skies on the two days following the May 7 sighting, and on both occasions he observed the similar red light. And on Friday, May 9, Paul Sanders witnessed the strange light with Diemert.

By this point, the RCMP had two witnesses with expertise in aviation to count on. Shelton was also an experienced pilot. He'd held his licence for almost a decade, knew how to identify an aircraft and worked with Metropolitan Investigation and Security, a local security firm at that time. Shelton's thoughts on the sighting mirrored Roberts.

As it happened, there was one other official witness, and this individual was a specialist in law enforcement.

Constable Nicholson was patrolling near Friendship Field around 12:15 AM on May 9 when he noticed a strange red light, just like the one Diemert had told him about in April. To get a better look, he stopped the car and got out.

>...[I] *saw an oval-shaped red light with an X-shaped background. The X-shaped light was white in colour, and not attached to the oval shape. In order to get a better view of the object, I then proceeded west on P.T.H. (Provincial Trunk Highway) 245, all the while keeping this red object in view. As I proceeded west on Hwy. 245 the object seemed to be flying in a north-westerly direction at an undetermined rate of speed. I continued west on PTH 245 for approximately 12 miles* [20 kilometres], *until I lost sight of the object over the trees.*

Constable Nicholson watched the object for a full 12 minutes, in his estimation, before it was finally too far away to see. Because the object was travelling in a northwesterly direction, toward Portage la Prairie, Nicholson called the town's rural detachment to see if they'd noticed anything in that area. They hadn't, which was disappointing. Still, Nicholson knew what he'd seen. Up to that point, only Diemert and his friends and associates had seen this strange light, and you couldn't really criticize if people thought the

entire scenario was nothing more than a hoax. Now—
well, it would be tough to argue that one of Carman's
finest was in on a hoax. Nicholson's testimony gave
the ongoing mystery added validity.

If the RCMP or the people of Carman thought they
might get a reprieve from the unusual stories, they were
mistaken. The reports continued throughout May,
with Diemert contacting the detachment with
another sighting, this time on May 13. Once again,
Diemert had several friends with him, and the story
was much the same.

There was a large, round light that was "bigger than
a car." It was red, soared between 150 and 275 metres
high and travelled between 135 and 150 kilometres per
hour. The light show continued for about 10 minutes.
No one involved in the sighting had been drinking, and
the light was first witnessed at the airfield.

A slight variance to the reports coming into the
station on that day were the stories filed by Howard
Bennett and Kerry McIntyre of Carman, as well as
Ted Story of Miami, Manitoba. Between 11:30 and
11:45 that evening, the three men were driving
together when they noticed an odd sight in the
Graysville area, 11 kilometres west of Carman.
According to their report, the object "was at or near
ground level and was tilted at an angle of approximately
45 degrees and was glowing red."

Around the same time, Allan Kerr of Winnipeg saw something when he was driving a couple of kilometres north of Carman. A cameraman for CKY-TV, Kerr managed to pull his gear from the car and shoot what he thought might have amounted to almost a half-minute of film before it was too far away. Sadly, the resulting video wasn't something investigators could use.

On June 27, Diemert and his wife were two of four residents who were involved in another sighting, this time at about 12:05 in the morning. Perhaps Diemert's tendency to work late into the midnight hours led him to so many sightings. Whatever the reason, he was front and centre, yet again. This time, however, the object was characterized by a "brilliant white strobe-type light which seemed to be revolving around the perimeter of another coloured light, red or blue, which was constant."

Report after report trickled into the Carman Detachment, and each one was forwarded to the National Research Council, but even after weeks and months had passed, no one had anything concrete to go on.

And then on July 7, there was a slight break in the investigation. Frederika Giesbrecht of Carman saw something that looked like what everyone in the area had been talking about over the last couple of months. Between 2:00 and 3:00 AM, she watched an object hovering in the sky 25 kilometres or so east of Carman. She took photos of it and called the Carman Detachment, filing a report with Corporal F.B. Savage. Again, the report was forwarded to a higher authority.

This time the detachment received a response: "From our analysis of her data, we conclude that the object which she photographed was the planet Jupiter, which was rising low in the east at that time."

The NRC returned the original photos but kept copies on file for their records. And it seems that not much more was said on the issue. So far, everyone was on board with the description of what they saw, but no one had any idea about how to identify the object—including the RCMP.

The sightings around Carman seemed to drop off slightly after July. At least the Diemerts and their acquaintances hadn't filed any further reports on the issue—until November 13. Robert was locking up the hangar at around 6:40 PM and getting ready to go home for supper when the red light appeared again, this time travelling from the northwest to the southeast. He knew right away the light was something he'd witnessed before—with a few twists, that is.

For one thing, more than one object was in the sky that night. A second craft appeared about 805 metres behind the first one that Robert, his wife and a man named Samuel Blackwell witnessed travelling "north to the Boyne River and then east towards Carman." The second object seemed to move on a north to south arc. Robert explained it this way to the RCMP:

At one point, the red lights on it went out for about ten seconds, and it shone a white light only. The red lights came on again, very bright, and I looked over my shoulder as I was running down the road to the house to get my binoculars, and the lights were pulsating.

And then a third light appeared, this one directly west of the three observers, turning sharply toward Winnipeg. "The closest it came to us would be about one mile [1.5 kilometres] or so. The size would be similar to that of a DC 8 or perhaps smaller. The shape appeared to be circular, spherical thing."

Many unexplained sightings remain just that— categorized as unexplained flying objects. But when it comes to the Carman sightings, it's unclear if there was ever an official investigation beyond the reports filed and interviews conducted at a local level. This is especially disturbing given that the sightings spanned the surrounding areas as well. Reports from Graysville, Lundar, Stephenfield, St. Claude, Roland, Sperling and Halbstadt supported the Carman sightings and spanned from the Diemerts' initial report to April 3, 1976, when the last report was filed.

It's not clear where the name Charlie Redstar came from either, but that's what the cluster of sightings is called. When it comes to the local folklore, some suggest Charlie Redstar was the UFO spotted in Carman, but that the subsequent and surrounding sightings were somehow connected, as if they were friends or relatives of the original UFO.

Some of the reports that had been filed were deemed the work of mischievous witnesses, or in other words, the work of an elaborate hoax. But for many of the folks living in or around Carman at that time, Charlie Redstar was as real as their neighbour, only far more mysterious. The sightings were never explained, nor did they continue after April 1976.

CHAPTER SIX

Saskatchewan

It was the darndest thing I've ever seen... It was very bright, it changed colours and it was about the size of the Moon. We watched it for ten minutes, but none of us could figure out what it was. One thing's for sure, I'll never make fun of people who say they've seen unidentified objects in the sky.... If I become President, I'll make every piece of information this country has about UFO sightings available to the public and the scientists...

—attributed to Jimmy Carter during the 1976 presidential campaign

Langenburg: A Flock of a Different Kind

TRESPASSING ON PRIVATE PROPERTY is never a good idea, and setting up a goose blind in the middle of a rapeseed field that's ready to harvest is just damn rude. The latest aluminum blinds are large enough to conceal hunters from the birds they are hunting. While these aluminum blinds helped out the hunter, they were no friends to Edwin Fuhr's rapeseed crop.

Frustrated by what he saw, the 36-year-old farmer stepped down off his swather, pulled the hood of his parka a little tighter over his head to protect himself from the light, icy-cold rain that had started to fall and, shuddering from the cold, started to make his way toward the shiny, circular object.

Fuhr was likely a little leery about approaching the strange object. If it was a goose or duck blind, there could be a hunter inside, ready with his rifle in hand, and the farmer certainly wouldn't want to startle someone with a gun. But he was bent on getting his swathing done. After all, it was the first of September, and he didn't want to push too far into the month— you can never tell when the weather will change and winter might blow in early.

He hadn't noticed the circular steel until he'd come up to within 15 metres of it, but he was determined to get whatever it was out of his way so he could finish his day's chores. As Fuhr moved closer and closer, it became evident that whatever was hanging out in his rapeseed field wasn't a duck blind—and it wasn't stationary either.

"I noticed the object was rotating, spinning (clockwise) and the grass around it was moving," Fuhr told reporters from one UFO magazine.

I stopped right there and viewed it for maybe two minutes. I don't know exactly how long I was standing there and instinct told me not to go any closer so I backed out all the way back to the swather, walked around it and got in on the left-hand side.

For the next 15 minutes Fuhr sat in his swather and watched as four more of these dome-shaped crafts flanked him on his other side. Fuhr admitted that he froze in fear. He didn't know what to do, so he didn't move. In fact, he could barely breathe as he watched all five objects rotate centimetres off the ground.

"Then they went straight up, all even, in a step formation," he continued. "They were up about 200 feet [60 metres] when a dark grey vapour appeared from the bottom two exhaust ports and lasted a few seconds. Then they were gone."

The entire experience unnerved the typically calm and easy-going Fuhr, and once the strange objects disappeared, the farmer rushed back to his farmhouse. His wife noticed something was wrong as soon as Fuhr stepped inside—she was doubly concerned when he told her what had occurred. Her husband's anxiety, the animated and disjointed way he relayed his tale, added to her concern.

The couple's unease continued throughout the day, and they were grateful when Edwin's sister and brother-in-law stopped by. Once again Fuhr told his story. Once again it was so outlandish that most folks sharing such a tale would be laughed at—but not Edwin. The man had a reputation for being reasonable, and everyone knew there was no way Fuhr would have made something like that up.

Anxious and unsettled though he was, Fuhr remained unconvinced that going to the authorities was a good idea. It would take his brother-in-law,

Karl Zorn, telephoning the local detachment later that night before the local RCMP learned of the curious case of the five unidentified flying objects soaring over Langenburg, Saskatchewan, that early September day in 1974.

The farmland of rural Saskatchewan is pretty predicable. Fields stretching out as far as the eye can see constitutes the typical geography. This is a province where farming dominates, and the human component in the equation takes a bit of a back seat. Small towns and villages dot the major roadways every 20 kilometres or so, and Langenburg is one of the last in a string of towns flanking the Yellowhead Highway between Saskatoon, 400 kilometres to the west, and the Manitoba border, another 10 kilometres to the east. False-front buildings typical of this prairie province line the highway, which pretty much goes through the centre of the community. And with less than 1000 people inhabiting this relatively new town, which was incorporated in 1959, Langenburg shares one other trait with every other town in Saskatchewan—when you live in Langenburg, like the old *Cheers* song goes, just about everybody knows your name.

Constable Ron Morier was on duty when Zorn telephoned the detachment and asked if the officers working that day had received any "calls reporting sightings of unidentified flying objects." Zorn's question

wasn't the kind of query that rolled into the office
every day, and there's no doubt it added some flavour
to what must have been an otherwise quiet Labour
Day Sunday evening. When Constable Morier told
Zorn there hadn't been any such calls, Zorn shared the
story Fuhr had told him earlier. Clearly, as outlandish
as it all must have seemed when Zorn first heard the
tale, Fuhr's obvious unease must have created an
equal measure of discomfort in Zorn's mind for him to
risk being laughed out of town by calling the police.

Once Zorn relayed Fuhr's experience to Constable
Morier, he went on to explain that Fuhr guessed the
"foreign sort of aircraft" ranged in size from about
2.5 to 3.5 metres in diameter. Zorn also told the officer
that Zorn had called his father-in-law about the strange
tale before calling the RCMP, and that it wasn't until
his father-in-law visited the location of the sightings
and returned with a description of "five definite circular
patterns left in swamp grass" that Zorn decided to take
the plunge and contact the authorities. If there was
something to Fuhr's experience, something potentially
dangerous, someone should be told about it.

Because Zorn's call hadn't come into the RCMP until
around 9:00 that Sunday evening, and the sun had
already set, Morier decided a visit to the farm would be
a waste of time at that hour. If he were pushed about the
issue, Constable Morier would have likely considered it
a waste of time under any circumstances. Still, Zorn's
tone had an eerie sense of urgency. There was also
another part of the equation to consider—a part of

Zorn's story that Morier had to agree on—and that was Fuhr's character. Various members of the detachment had known Fuhr for the previous four years and not once during that time was he "known to materialize any such stories." In his report, Morier stated that Fuhr was "a responsible person."

Following his investigation into the story, Morier would add that the information Fuhr provided was "considered reliable."

The problem the authorities now faced was to gather every small detail they could, and hopefully some physical evidence to support those details, and launch an investigation into the obvious question that would fuel coffee chatter for months and years to come. What exactly happened that fresh September morning on a farm a scant 10 kilometres from town, and was this odd encounter something that could threaten the peaceful existence of folks in this northern Saskatchewan town?

On the morning of September 2, Constable Morier accompanied Zorn to the Fuhr farm. While Morier was initially skeptical about what he would see once he got there, the officer's tone changed on seeing the circular patterns forming the shape of a horseshoe in the middle of Fuhr's rapeseed field. The officer pulled out his

measuring tape and began recording the particulars at
the scene:

> *There were five different distinct circles, caused by*
> *something exerting what had to be heavy air or exhaust*
> *pressure over the high grass. The grass was flattened in*
> *a clockwise circle with the flattened portion being*
> *approx. 18 in.* [45 centimetres]. *The total diameter of*
> *two of the circles was 12 ft.* [3.5 metres], *with the other*
> *three being approx 10½ ft.* [3 metres] *in diameter. The*
> *grass in the centre portion of the ring was standing,*
> *and appeared untouched. Photographs were taken of*
> *the rings. Fuhr stated that he was so involved with*
> *swathing in the rape, which was a good 3½ ft.* [one
> metre] *tall, that he didn't notice one of the "Saucers"*
> *located in the sunken dried slough in the field until he*
> *was about 50 ft.* [15 metres] *away from them.*

Morier bent down to examine how the rapeseed
lay on the ground and to see any configuration it
made; he even pressed his nose to the ground to see
if any odour was left behind. He then had to rely on
Fuhr's description of the "saucers" for other details
such as their colour and height. Fuhr estimated the
crafts to be between 1 and 1.5 metres in height, and
they were "highly polished steel, with the bottom lip
being a duller steel shade."

When asked, Fuhr said he didn't remember seeing
any windows or lights. However, the saucers were
spinning at a high speed, so fast that had Fuhr not
noticed the grass moving beneath them, he might
have thought they were stationary. Such high-speed

spinning could certainly have prevented him from seeing windows. And the highly polished steel could have camouflaged lights on the crafts, if there had indeed been any.

There were two other strange facts to consider about Fuhr's encounter. Despite the apparent rapid movement of the crafts, he didn't hear any noise. Also, the crops surrounding the impressions on the ground were the only markings. The rest of the field was completely untouched. The scene was as unexplainable as the story, and even a skeptic like Morier had to admit it was starting to look like aliens may have visited Langenburg after all.

Morier filed his report with his local detachment. A copy was also forwarded to the Upper Atmosphere Research Section of the Astrophysics Branch of the National Research Council in Ottawa. Until another sighting was reported, or someone came forward with additional information, the RCMP couldn't do much more. Still, the eerie feeling that people in the area had didn't subside for some time. The story even hit the *Saskatoon Star-Phoenix* on September 18, and according to that report, folks were still fretting over the encounter. "Some farmers are afraid to work their fields," Constable Morier told reporters. "At least that's what I hear on coffee row."

As of this writing, almost four decades later, an explanation for the strange floating objects in Langenburg has remained elusive. The Fuhrs still live in the area, and Edwin's story still makes its way along the grapevine.

He has even been profiled on several television shows that highlight strange unsolved mysteries. And in many ways, the longevity of interest in the story is no surprise. After all, when it comes to UFO sightings, the region surrounding Langenburg is a bit of a hotbed.

There are several reasons why the story of the rings in the Fuhr rapeseed field has continued to intrigue the public, and they begin with Dr. Allen McNamara, head of the National Research Council's Upper Atmosphere Research Centre at the time. On September 26, McNamara told reporters with the *Saskatoon Star-Phoenix* that he had an answer about what happened in Fuhr's field, and it was all about mushrooms.

McNamara said that a type of underground mushroom that often grows in a circular pattern could have produced what he called "fairy rings" in the farmer's field. He went on to explain that several kinds of mushrooms could produce the rings—some research suggests as many as 60 species can sprout suddenly in this pattern, their flat tops hovering a few centimetres above the ground. Many of these species have also been known to emit what McNamara described as a luminous glow. "There are whole lists of mushrooms which glow in the ground which produce a bioluminescence," he told reporters. "It's possible some of these could cause fairy rings."

The article also explained that some mushrooms had indeed been discovered beneath the flattened rapeseed, but that no attention had been paid to them because investigators didn't see how they might have been connected to the phenomenon. To the average layperson, the idea made no sense whatsoever. But McNamara also stated that the crushed crop could have been "the result of dead grass [from the mushrooms] being pushed over by the wind."

McNamara's theory might have answered his questions and the questions on the minds of many of his peers, but it fell short as far as other researchers were concerned. For one thing, the flattened circles in Edwin's fields were a lot thicker than the circles that would have been left behind by a sudden eruption of mushrooms, which tend to sprout in a single-file formation. The mushroom theory also didn't explain the 1- to 1.5-metre vessels that Edwin believed were hovering over his field or the fact that he saw them lift off the ground, and then disappear into the clouds.

Dr. Al Hyneck, head of the UFO centre at Northern University in Chicago, argued that the rings resembled photographs of similar impressions he'd seen from several other countries, all of which had remained unexplained.

Another researcher also discounted the mushroom explanation. Dr. Gruen suggested that the glow from the mushrooms would have been visible to the farmer in the daylight, though he did concede "rotting vegetation in a nearby slough could have produced patches of mist."

Most of the residents living around Langenburg didn't buy any of these pat answers to a complicated problem. They were still convinced there was more to Fuhr's sighting than a bunch of wild fungus.

And by the time the Saskatoon *Star-Phoenix* ran the story on the findings from the National Research Council, news of another sighting was starting to make its round in the area and battling for recognition in the media.

Edwin Fuhr may have had a stellar reputation in his community, but a resident with an equally impressive character and official credentials reported another sighting not all that far away, in Martensville.

About 6500 people inhabit Martensville, about 20 kilometres north of Saskatoon. Today it's considered one of the fastest-growing communities in Saskatchewan, recording an astounding 25-percent growth in the five years between the 1996 census and the 2001 census. In fact, the town's official website states that the "city" of Martensville has grown so fast that "mailboxes have been placed into some of the residential areas." But back in 1974 it was considerably smaller; it was incorporated as a village in 1966, and in 1969, that designation changed to town status. So while

Martensville was growing rapidly, at that particular point in its history, it was still quaint and friendly—a place where everyone did know your name.

And everyone certainly knew Albert and Zenia Goddue.

As the town constable, Albert had a high profile in town. He was stalwart and sensible—a no-nonsense kind of guy. So when he and his wife went to the Saskatoon *Star-Phoenix* with their story of a strange sighting they said occurred on Thursday, September 26, anyone in the community who heard about it, along with folks in communities for many miles around, took notice.

Constable Goddue was off duty when he and his wife were doing a bit of shopping in the early evening. Albert had pulled up in front of Ford's Pharmacy on Avenue H. South, and he stayed inside the car while Zenia ran inside to pick up a few necessities. Albert might have been flipping through the radio channels or flipping through the pages of the *Star-Phoenix*. Or maybe he was sitting idly, humming to himself and thinking about what the next day at work might bring. But at some point he paused; perhaps something caught his eye. And he looked up into the sky. That's when he noticed a "craft moving in an 'arc' from the southwest."

Albert watched as the craft hung suspended in the air. "I didn't have my watch, but I would say it hovered for quite a while...perhaps five minutes," he told reporters later.

Albert really wasn't sure what to make of his sighting. The logical explanations didn't ring true; at least whatever was soaring across the sky didn't look like any airplane he was familiar with. He'd have to ask his wife what she thought—if she made it back to the car before the object vanished.

He was surprised when Zenia returned to the car in time to share his sighting; she was surprised when he told her to look out the window and watch the night sky.

Zenia immediately noticed what her husband was pointing out. Both she and Albert described what could only have been an aircraft that looked like an "upside down saucer, or like a parachute, with a flat bottom and a domed top" and "no visible means of propulsion, no tail or propellers, and no noise."

At first the object looked like it was moving slowly, but as it continued in a southerly direction, it appeared to pick up speed. And though there weren't any distinctive visible markings that either Zenia or her husband noticed, Albert described it as being "bright aluminum" in colour. He also said that even though some daylight still remained, the object was "glowing brighter than the Northern Star."

As with all such reports, air traffic controllers—in this case those at the nearby Saskatoon airport—were contacted to see if they'd seen any unexplained blips on their radar. They had not. They did have a theory, though. They suggested that what the Goddues had seen was nothing more than an "aircraft landing with its lights on." Albert vehemently disagreed with that assessment and insisted "it was like nothing I have ever seen in the sky before."

With the kind of year Saskatchewan was having in regards to strange sightings, most folks who heard the Goddues' story were inclined to believe that something weird was going on.

It wasn't only in the northern part of the province that residents had witnessed unusual sights in the sky that same year. Farther south, near the U.S. border, at about 7:45 on the morning of February 8, Donald Davidson received a phone call from his neighbour Hugh Brawley: the Davidson and Brawley families lived about 20 kilometres south of McCord at that time. It appears that Hugh had noticed an object in the sky farther south of their location and wanted his neighbour's take on the issue.

Davidson grabbed his field glasses and went outside to scan the horizon. Because of its unique nature, the object in question wasn't difficult to find. Davidson later said that what he saw in the sky that day "appeared oblong with a cone-shaped object descending from the bottom." Davidson's wife also noticed the craft but thought it looked more circular than her husband suggested. The couple did agree on the colour: it was "a luminous white."

At 8:20 that morning, after watching the object since Brawley phoned the Davidson residence, Donald decided to report the sighting to the Mankota Detachment of the RCMP. He and his wife then continued to watch the craft until about 9:00 AM, when it finally disappeared.

Constable D. Feather first interviewed Davidson and then contacted Brawley to hear his version of the sighting. Brawley's story concurred in every respect with what Davidson had shared, even though Brawley didn't have the advantage of using field glasses. Because the Brawley home was a few kilometres north of the Davidsons' residence, from his perspective, the object "appeared to be sitting on the horizon." According to Brawley, the "object had risen in four stages and remained still for approx. 20 minutes before ascending to the southeast."

Once Feather had secured independent statements from the two men, he called another area resident named Richard Couture. Because Couture was driving a school bus in the same general vicinity where Brawley and Davidson noticed the unexplained phenomenon in the sky, Feather thought that perhaps Couture might have noticed something as well. And he was right. Couture did report seeing a "bright light in the southeast." He couldn't tell what exactly was producing that bright light, but he had noted the time: it was about 7:20 in the morning.

Constable Feather closed his report by stating all three witnesses were reliable, reputable members of society. He then forwarded the report to the Astrophysics Branch of the Upper Atmosphere Research Centre at the National Research Council. And as far as strange objects hovering over the McCord District, that appeared to be the end of the story.

But the subject of UFO sightings in Saskatchewan that autumn was far from over.

Some time between 8:45 and 9:00 PM on September 17, James Kolenz, his brother Robert and their friend Loretta Thompson spotted a strange hoverer near Roche Percee. It was a clear night, and the last warm vestiges of summer were keeping the crisp, autumn air typical of that time of year at bay. The three young people were out for a stroll when they noticed an egg-shaped object hovering about 100 metres directly overhead. It remained suspended for several minutes before it finally moved.

To the three observers, it looked as though a "short pointed tail" protruded at one end, and a "yellowish green light" attached to the end of the tail continued blinking on and off. The three watched the object and its flashing tail end for about 10 minutes. During that time, it moved "north in circles, in an easterly direction in zig-zags and then went due north" over the neighbouring community of Bienfait before it disappeared.

James filed a report with Corporal A. Myshrall of the Estevan Detachment, but it doesn't seem as though any follow-up was done on that particular sighting. However, it was only one of many reports of strange sights in the night sky in the southern part of the province. A little farther northwest, near the community of Lang, Weyburn resident Fred Erickson was driving northwest along Highway 39 when he spotted an odd sight hovering in an otherwise clear sky. Curious, Erickson pulled onto the shoulder near another idling vehicle and got out of his car, hoping for a better look. The driver of the other vehicle had the same idea, and the two men stood there, eyes lifted to the heavens, and wondered what they were witnessing.

It appears that Erickson was the only individual to report what he saw that night to the Milestone Detachment because the second witness is labelled as "unidentified" in the police report. What Erickson described were actually two objects "shaped like [an] inverted saucer with [a] bump [on the] top." He said the saucers were about 18 metres in diameter, and they "seemed to be [the] same in height." Erickson went on to explain that the crafts were silver—at least that's what it looked like from his vantage point— but he did not see any glow or obvious light.

While one of the crafts held back at a distance, the other hovered nearby. Aside from its unidentifiable appearance, the craft's behaviour demanded attention. Erickson said that when he moved his vehicle, the object also moved. When he stopped, the object appeared to hover above him. Whatever the craft was, it interfered with his AM radio reception, and his two-way radio "stopped receiving and only hummed." Erickson said he was familiar with aircraft, and whatever was hovering at a 45-degree angle overhead was certainly no plane.

The day before Erickson's sighting, the Milestone Detachment had received a call from James Pearce of Wilcox, another community northwest of Milestone. Pearce also noted a "saucer like" UFO moving from east to west. He watched the object for about 10 minutes, but the craft he saw had several coloured, blinking lights. In this case, though, officers blamed the unexplained craft on aerial training exercises at the nearby Canadian Forces Base in Moose Jaw. After Erickson called the same detachment, officers decided to reconnect with Pearce and ask if he thought their assessment of the matter was possible. Pearce vehemently denied the possibility that what he'd seen that night was an aircraft.

Not everyone calls the police with information about a UFO they've spotted. For one thing, some folks might think the police won't take them seriously or that the authorities wouldn't waste their time investigating something so intangible as a UFO when they had crimes to solve and speeders to catch. On the other hand, what did the RCMP know about the subject anyway? If someone really believed they'd seen something that needed an explanation and had a keen interest in that sighting, they might consider reporting it to another authority.

In 1974, the National UFO Reporting Center opened in Seattle, Washington, and provided a hotline phone number to receive reports on "unusual aerial phenomena." Almost immediately the centre gained a solid reputation for unbiased research, and even police departments were known to direct residents who'd claimed to witness sightings to the organization.

In the autumn of 1974, a youngster living in Saskatoon noticed something odd while he and two of his friends were sitting on the roof of his parents' home smoking a cigarette. It was between 8:00 and 9:00 PM. All three lads were lying on the roof, hands behind their heads and staring off into the night sky when a triangular object whirled into their line of vision. "It was a perfect triangle with a white light on each point of the triangle," the boy stated in his report. "There were trails coming off the back two points of the triangle. The triangle was pitch black and blocked out the stars above it as it flew over top of me."

Although he couldn't provide an estimate on how many metres in the air the object was, he estimated it was as high as a jetliner would have been travelling.

For a moment the boy considered the possibility that the object was some kind of meteor, but that didn't make sense since it "blocked out the stars above [him] as it flew over top." It also moved rather slowly—too slow to be a meteor, as far as he was concerned.

Even though the youngsters were obviously engaging in behaviour that would have been frowned upon, and they might have eliminated the detail of exactly where they were when they witnessed the triangular object, all three rushed into the house to report the sighting. After hearing what he had to say, the young man's parents called the Saskatoon Airport to share the story and inquire if there'd been any other similar reports called in that night. To that point there hadn't been, and the family didn't pursue other lines of inquiry.

Either no one else observed the strange phenomenon or no one bothered to report it, and the story remained little more than a childhood memory. Several years later, the unnamed witness contacted the National UFO Reporting Centre with what he saw—and it was as fresh in his mind as it had been the night it happened.

UFO sightings aren't an anomaly in Saskatchewan. Nor is the occurrence of clusters of sightings unusual. But in 1989, what Sergeant Herman Fogen referred to as an "outbreak" of unidentified sightings did make a unique story in the UFO world. In fact, the many sightings were so compelling that the Regina *Leader-Post* ran a special series of articles in their November 4 edition.

Being posted in the Langenburg Detachment, Fogen was well aware of Edwin Fuhr's UFO sighting, which had stymied the police department and frightened farmers out of their fields. Fifteen years had passed, and Fuhr's strange sighting in 1974 was still fresh in everyone's mind.

Fogen wasn't unfamiliar with reports of UFO sightings of his own. Before his arrival in Langenburg, Fogen had been posted at the detachment based in the small town of Bengough, south of Regina. When he experienced his first UFO sighting report, he was checking out something altogether unrelated. It was a story he heard in passing—a one-in-a-million sighting that, although strange, wasn't significantly compelling to force in-depth scrutiny.

The story he heard was about a group of young teens out for an evening walk down the streets of Langenburg around 7:00 PM on October 11, two days after Thanksgiving. They noticed a string of strange, coloured lights that they thought might have been shooting stars or an airplane. But as the craft got closer to them, it was clear this was no plane.

"It was like dishes put together, a saucer," 13-year-old Todd Weinheimer told reporters.

Rather than running for cover, thinking they'd seen a spaceship, the teens started waving the skateboards they'd been cruising the sidewalks on, trying to attract the attention of whomever or whatever might be piloting the craft. Initially, the ship hovered about 120 metres overhead, but when it dropped suddenly to between 30 and 60 metres, it frightened the boys and they scrambled for cover. Although each of the boys were watching from a slightly different vantage point, their stories and descriptions were remarkably consistent, from the shape of the craft and its erratic flight pattern to the blue, red, orange, yellow and white lights that flickered over its body.

Despite the young ages of the witnesses, officers at the Langenburg RCMP considered the boys to be reliable and genuine, and didn't believe they were trying to gain a little mischievous attention by making up a bizarre tale. Still, had that been the only report, it might not have garnered quite as much interest as it did; however, as the days and weeks passed, several independent reports of strange sightings started trickling in to the local police office.

While the sighting relayed by the young boys took place in the evening, a time when strange lights appearing in the sky are more noticeable, another sighting took place in the early morning hours of Friday, October 13. But it wasn't bright lights or loud noises that caught Rose Neumeier's attention; it was just a feeling that she needed to look up and take notice.

Rose was talking on the telephone when something she couldn't initially describe caught her eye. She was sitting in her kitchen, gazing outside the window as she chatted with her friend when, according to the police report, a "bright flash of light struck her eyes and lit up the whole kitchen." At first she thought the glare was the result of the sun reflecting off the "windshield of a car travelling down the grid road south of the farm." But the road was too far away, and any glare off a windshield wouldn't have been powerful enough to cause such a shocking light.

Blinking away the brightness, Rose scanned the family's farmyard for some explanation for what she saw. Her eyes rested slightly above the family's garage—where she noticed a strange, "oblong-shaped silver object" suspended above the roof. As in the story shared by the group of young skateboarders two days earlier, the craft looked like "two pie plates thrust together," and the glaring light was either glare from a "bright silver band around its middle" or a result of the sun reflecting off the shiny shell.

Separated by nothing more than a windowpane and a single wall, Rose felt threatened by the closeness of the unknown entity. She guessed the object was about as wide across as the length of their 9-metre garage. It didn't make a sound—even the Neumeiers' dogs and the herd of cattle grazing near the family's corral weren't alerted to its presence. And then as suddenly as it appeared, the craft was gone. The entire episode lasted only a few minutes, and although Rose shared her experience with her friends and family, she wasn't about to go public with it.

But you know what they say about best-laid plans.

That same day, families living in some of the other farmsteads near the Neumeier farm had called the RCMP with a concern that there were poachers in the area. Following up on the complaint, Sergeant Fogen drove up to the Neumeier farm about 4:30 PM and knocked on the door. Rose couldn't hide her surprise at seeing the officer, even though his presence had caused a cacophony of barking and bawling from the Neumeiers' dogs and cattle.

"Who told you?" she asked the officer.

Sergeant Fogen informed her that one of her neighbours complained about hearing gunshots in the area. Without a second thought, Rose blurted out that she thought the officer was there about the UFO she'd seen that morning. And the next thing Fogen knew, he was taking down another statement, this time about an unexplained aerial phenomenon, along with details about the Neumeiers' farm. He noted that the Neumeiers' rural homestead was considerably isolated, almost vanishing from view from certain vantage points in the undulating landscape.

Rose's story must have seemed incredible. However, that Sergeant Fogen placed a great deal of credence in the tale, and almost concluded that the Langenburg area was being visited by some foreign or alien presence, is evident in one statement he made to reporters: "Of all the farms in this area, why did they pick on [the] Neumeiers?"

In the early evening hours of October 18, Colin Rosin and his nine-year-old daughter spotted what they believed was a UFO. The father-daughter duo was driving along Highway 8, between Esterhazy and Langenburg, talking about the many strange happenings in the area in the previous few weeks when Colin spotted something out of the corner of his eye.

"There was something just coasting across the sky over top of my car that had two beautiful blue flashing lights, two red flashing lights and what I think was sort of yellowish or whitish lights," Rosin told reporters from the Regina *Leader-Post*. The lights gave him the "same impression as if you had those lights recessed into your ceiling in a house."

Colin and his daughter weren't frightened by what they saw, even though Rosin was adamant the aircraft "wasn't any plane." He even stopped the car and watched as the object hovered overhead. And throughout the experience, Colin couldn't help but remember back to the time when he was a teenager and saw an "oblong shape" he described as "greyish silver" in colour flashing a sequence of lights in the sky.

Like Rose Neumeier, Rosin had no intention of going public with his sighting, mostly because he didn't have a photograph of the object. But he did share his story with a few friends, one of whom knew someone who knew someone with the CBC—or at least that's what Rosin believed was the reason behind the sequence of events that led to reporters calling at his door. In all honesty, Rosin couldn't blame the media for its interest.

"There's been some pretty weird things going on around Langenburg this last little while and it kind of makes you wonder," he said.

The rush of sightings in and around the Langenburg area in 1989 refuelled an already keen interest in UFOs among residents. To this day, Saskatchewan continues to be a hotbed of activity for unexplained phenomena.

CHAPTER SEVEN

Nova Scotia

Something came down there, there's no doubt about it…I'm not sure what it was. It's made me wonder, ya'know, way out there in space, if there's some other type of life besides us…Whatever that object was, it come from somewhere and our authorities don't know anything about it, so they're saying.

–Lawrence Smith, Nova Scotia fisherman

Shag Harbour: Power in Numbers

HIGHWAY 3 WINDS ITS WAY ALONG a good portion of the southern coast of Nova Scotia. Parts of the highway border the Atlantic Ocean so closely that if you had a yearning to, you could quite likely toss a stone onto its shore when driving by without much difficulty. Small villages like Shag Harbour—which are typically equipped with a post office, boat docks, a couple of churches, a bed and breakfast or two, perhaps a school, and if they're lucky, a police detachment, along with a few hundred residents—line the shores. From just about anywhere along the southern tip of the province, a misty-blue sky appears to meet the deeper blue of the ocean. The salty sea air is invigorating, the scene strangely alluring.

Since French colonists first settled in Nova Scotia in the early 1600s, and throughout its colourful history, the residents of Canada's second smallest province have relied on the sea for their sustenance and livelihood. Even since the collapse of the cod stocks, fishing continues to be a way of life in this part of our country, with lobster being one of the mainstays of the current economy.

That said, fishing is a dangerous job. The Atlantic is cold, unpredictable and deadly, and most residents living in the small villages dotting the coastline have lost a friend or family member to its merciless grasp. This common dependence on the sea and the collective grief it sometimes causes help form the strong bonds between the few hundred people who live in Shag Harbour.

So when an RCMP officer called Lawrence Smith at around 11:00 PM on the night of October 4, 1967, asking the 34-year-old fisherman if he could take his boat out into the sound to help with a possible rescue mission, Lawrence didn't hesitate. The officer explained that there had been reports of some kind of aircraft crashing into the ocean, just a kilometre or so off shore, and the RCMP were recruiting a number of boat owners to go to the scene. If there were any truth to those reports, finding possible survivors would be completely dependent on the speed with which a rescue operation could be organized and dispatched.

Lawrence gathered his gear and rushed out the door as soon as he hung up the phone. By the time he arrived at the wharf, a crowd had already gathered, and several people were actual eyewitnesses to the event. The bits and pieces of chatter Lawrence could snatch from one group or another only added to the intensity of the scene playing out in the water before them. For Lawrence, the memory of that night would never fade from memory.

Forty years has done nothing to dim the memory of what Laurie Wickens saw that cool fall night in 1967. What he'd witnessed was as vividly imprinted in his mind four decades later as it had been that night when he was just 18 years old and driving with a couple of friends to Shag Harbour from his home near Bear Point. Wickens told reporters from the Canadian Press, in 2007:

> One light would come on, then two, then three, then four, then they'd all go out for a second, then they'd repeat. It seemed to be going along with us for, I don't know, three or four minutes, while we were driving up to Middle Shag Harbour…As we started to make the corner, the lights, instead of flying level, they started flying maybe a 45-degree angle down towards

the water. We (were) at the bottom of the hill, and we only lost sight of it for a few seconds and when we made the top of the hill, the light was in the water.

The story of each witness was the same: a row of lights flickered and hovered in the sky and then plunged into the Atlantic with a "high whistling sound," hitting the water with such force that it sounded like an explosion. The consistency of stories among the people who had witnessed the event from a variety of locations propelled what is now known as the Shag Harbour Incident into the public arena. Those stories were also a primary reason why the circumstances of that night garnered so much attention from various authorities.

Another good reason for that attention was that one of those eyewitnesses was an RCMP officer.

A memo entitled "UFO Report, Lower Wood Harbour, NS," penned by W.W. Turner, Colonel and Director of Operations, and dated October 6, 1967, explained that RCMP corporal Werbicki of the nearby Barrington Passage Detachment was one of seven witnesses initially identified as having seen the UFO hovering above the water, and then watching it crash.

In his memo, Turner describes the object as being "in excess of 60 feet [18 metres] in diameter" with "four white lights spaced horizontally at a distance of 15 feet [4.5 metres]." According to Turner, "the object, flying in an easterly direction when first sighted, descended rapidly into the water and produced a bright flash on impact. One light remained on the surface for considerable time but sank before a boat could reach it."

Turner then stated that the "Rescue Co-ordination Centre conducted [a] preliminary investigation and discounted the possibilities that the sighting was produced by an aircraft, flares, floats or any other known objects."

Constable Ron Pound was another officer who saw the strange object in the sky. Pound was patrolling Highway 3 and travelling toward Shag Harbour when the crash occurred. By the time he reached the shore near the crash site, Corporal Werbicki and Constable Ron O'Brien were on their way from the Barrington Passage Detachment. From the shore, all three officers saw something floating on the water, but the distance between the object and the shoreline made it difficult for anyone to tell if what they were seeing was an object or a light emanating from the sinking aircraft.

With so many people corroborating each other's stories, it was impossible to deny that something had happened that defied logical explanation. The night was clear and the waters calm. If a plane had crashed into the Atlantic, it certainly couldn't have been blamed on the weather.

It wasn't long before a hole would be punched in the plane-crash theory. Officers contacted the Joint Rescue Co-ordination Centre in Halifax, as well as military facilities throughout Nova Scotia, to discover if anyone had received any calls for help or had knowledge of any missing aircraft. The answers were the same at every call—there was no knowledge of any missing aircraft, civilian or military.

While the investigation was proceeding, the results of every theory tested returned more questions than answers. By this point it was clear that whatever dropped into the harbour was not a plane. But what was it?

When Laurie Wickens called the Barrington Passage RCMP to make his initial report, the first question the officer on duty asked him was if he'd been drinking. Wickens said he hadn't, and if the officer taking the call had any doubt, it was soon removed when a steady stream of calls started rolling into the detachment. One such report might warrant a question of alcohol consumption, but as the reports accumulated, and there wasn't a mid-week holiday providing residents with a reason to throw a wild party, the idea of callers being under the influence was increasingly unlikely.

Because no one could offer any explanation about what actually crashed that night, it was imperative that officials treated the situation as a rescue mission. Until concrete answers were forthcoming, the authorities had to assume there could be survivors. Vehicles gathered at the scene had been lined up along the shoreline where the alleged crash had occurred, shining their high beams into the dark night to provide boaters with some light in the absence of a full moon. Smith steered his vessel into the harbour, pushing his motor to go as fast as it could, while a couple of his buddies and an RCMP officer who had accompanied him scanned the water for survivors, suitcases, bits of wreckage or anything else that might help identify the "dark object," as it was referred to by several witnesses. Despite the fact that the authorities had pretty much ruled out an aircraft crash, witnesses still believed that was what they had seen. At the same time, most folks agreed that if it was an aircraft, it wasn't a type that any of them had ever seen before.

Members of the RCMP and officials with the military directed the fishing boats searching the bay. The Canadian Coast Guard Lifeboat 101 also joined in the effort. For hours the boats and their crews trolled back and forth searching the area stretching from the shoreline to a kilometre or so out into the water. Neither debris nor survivors were found. "All we found was a patch of yellowish brown foam on the water—the colour looked like burnt pancakes to me, you know when they're good and brown," Smith told Canadian Press reporters in 2001. "It was a strip of foam that looked like a runway to me, where something come *[sic]* down on the water and sunk or the lights went out and it lifted off again." In 1967, Captain Bradford Shand told reporters with the Halifax *Chronicle-Herald* that the "strange foam" was "at least

80 feet wide [24.5 metres]" and "yellowish in colour."
He said he'd "never seen anything like it before."

No one could explain the strange foam. It was the
only physical evidence to support the belief that
anything at all had occurred, so it was inconceivable
that no one involved in the investigation thought to
take a sample of the weird slick. However, the fact
that this foam definitely had existed added more
credibility to the story of a downed craft. Clearly
a deeper investigation into the event was in order.
In a desperate quest to locate something "concrete"
before it was swept away to sea, the Royal Canadian Air
Force searched from the air while the Canadian navy
based in Grandby sent a four-man dive team to scour
the ocean floor. Officials in Halifax sent another
three divers to the scene. If there was something to
be discovered, it was going to be found.

By now it was pretty clear to the officials involved
in the investigation that they were dealing with
a bona fide UFO sighting—if you consider a UFO
simply as an unidentified flying object that is not
necessarily extraterrestrial. If, as some were suggesting,
an otherworldly spacecraft had invaded the earth's
atmosphere near Shag Harbour, this might be one time
when concrete, irrefutable evidence that intelligent
life from another planet does exist could be retrieved.
Officials weren't cutting corners when it came to

bringing in every tool to ensure the search was successful, including the latest in metal detection devices.

Meanwhile, local fishermen were also anxious to get
some answers. Most of them had to pass through the
crash site daily on their way to their fishing grounds,
and the events of October 4 had made them all more
than a little leery. And even though officials had
gone on record saying no debris had been recovered,
some fishermen believed they'd seen divers pulling
shiny bits of something out of the water. No one was
admitting to finding any evidence, so if the fishermen
had indeed seen something, then there could only be
one explanation—someone was trying to cover
something up.

The question was why?

In their book *Dark Object: The World's Only Government-
Documented UFO Crash*, published in 2001, Don Ledger
and Chris Styles explain the official stance was that
the water search came up empty. "By 10:20 AM, the
Rescue Command Centre in Halifax was referring to
the object as a UFO, having eliminated the possibility
that it was a crashed airplane."

From a front-page story in the Halifax *Chronicle-
Herald* dated Monday, October 9, 1967, a worried
public learned that divers were being pulled from the
bay and the formal investigation into the strange
happenings of October 4 had been terminated. In the
article, a spokesperson from the Canadian Forces
Maritime Command went on record saying that after
spending three days scouring the ocean floor, the

seven divers hadn't found a thing: "Not a trace...not a clue...not a bit of anything."

While an official explanation about what actually happened that October night never materialized, plenty of theories were being pondered in the minds of Shag Harbour residents and officials alike. In particular, the fact that the incident occurred so close to CFB Shelburne, a military facility located about 50 kilometres from the alleged crash site, was of utmost interest.

At that time, the United States Navy and other North American Treaty Organization (NATO) countries had been establishing SOSUS (SOund SUrveillance System) technology. The main purpose of SOSUS technology was to monitor the movement of Russian submarines. Six initial locations were chosen, southern Nova Scotia being one of those choices. The original HMCS *Shelburne*, located in Sandy Point, was operated under the guise of an "Oceanographic Research Station" when in fact it was actually the "first SOSUS station in Canada."

Was it possible that the unidentified object spotted flying near Shag Harbour had anything to do with any military operations CFB Shelburne might have been involved in? Did the fallout from Cold War tensions— the countless military manoeuvres, technological competitiveness, endless propaganda and the world of secret agents and espionage—have anything to do with the Shag Harbour Incident? Could tensions between the Western world and the Soviet Union and its allies have resulted in the production of some kind of high-tech military device?

At least one authority from the National Research Council of Canada went on record saying that the Shag Harbour UFO could have actually been some kind of "secret war machine" from the United States. An article dated October 13, 1967, quoted Professor Rupert MacNeill as one notable scientist who thought there was some merit to the possibility that the U.S. had perfected a machine that could "travel by air, sea, and beneath the sea."

"I feel these are real things," MacNeill told reporter David Bentley. "I have had a number of reports over the last couple of years...I know nothing for sure, but from what I have heard and seen, it seems to me they might be experimental craft of some kind."

If indeed the U.S. had developed such a versatile vehicle, it made perfect sense to MacNeill that it was being kept confidential. "After all, they are in a competition for survival," he said.

In response to reports like that of the Shag Harbour Incident, a technical committee charged with further investigation was struck at the University of Toronto Institute for Aerospace Studies. In 1967, Professor Tennyson was the acting chairman of the committee responsible for researching "Unidentified Atmospheric

Phenomena." Tennyson agreed with MacNeill that it was possible the unidentified dark object hovering over Shag Harbour had been a "new supercraft under test." At the same time, he wasn't averse to the idea that the UFO was indeed something alien.

"...I do believe in unidentified atmospheric phenomena. Whether it happens to be an extraterrestrial vehicle, a military machine or what—I think we should try to find out," Tennyson told reporters.

Official records show there had been a flurry of UFO sightings in the area in 1967. Many of the reports took place before or after the October 4 event, but others happened the same day. At about 7:15 PM, Captain Pierre Charbeneau and First Officer Robert Ralph were piloting Air Canada Flight 305 over Québec when they noticed a light to the east that was "bigger and brighter than surrounding stars." Over the next several moments the pilots watched as the light grew, changed colour and then exploded into what looked like a fireball.

Much closer to home but still more than 160 kilometres from the crash site, Darrell Dorey explained how he and his mother and sister saw from their home in Mahone Bay "a yellowish sphere and an oval shaped cloudish thing" hovering in the sky.

One of the more lengthy sightings was likely that of Leo Howard Mersey. At about 9:00 PM, the captain of a fishing vessel was sailing about 51.5 kilometres south of the Sombro Lighthouse when he noticed an object about 25.5 kilometres northeast of his location. Because he knew the Canadian navy practiced in the area, he didn't give the sighting much thought initially. But as time wore on he thought it increasingly odd, especially when he learned about what was happening near Shag Harbour. On October 7, he contacted the Halifax RCMP and filed the following statement:

...At the same time there were three other objects on the radar and about 6 miles [9.5 kilometres] from the first object. I would say it disappeared about 11:00 PM, when it went up in the air. I could not see any shape or form to it because of the distance. When it went into the air it only had one flashing light. While the object was on the water, or close to the water, it had three real bright flashing red lights. All the lights on it were red. I could not see any lights on the other three objects as they were only appearing on the radar. It is not unusual to see the Navy, or aircraft, dropping things into the water there. I had never seen anything like that before but it sounds like the thing they are looking for down off Shelburne or Barrington Passage. When the object left it went straight up in the air with only one red light.

Clearly Mersey still believed there was a logical, and likely military, explanation for the Shag Harbour Incident. In an effort to diffuse those beliefs, the

Department of National Defence (DND) flatly denied any knowledge of a "secret experiment going on in the United States or elsewhere that would explain the Shelburne UFO" in a short front-page Halifax *Chronicle-Herald* article dated October 13.

But where did that leave the residents of Shag Harbour and the rest of the province?

Many years later, in their book *Dark Object*, Ledger and Styles explored the idea that two objects might have been involved in the alleged crash. The men recounted a tale shared by a Montréal woman named Ms. Fountain. The day after her father, Wayne Nickerson, read the news article about the Shag Harbour Incident, he told his family about seeing "two moon-like lights" that same night. At the time, the Nickersons lived in Pubnico, about 32 kilometres northwest of Shag Harbour, and Wayne was travelling to Woods Harbour from Shag Harbour. At one point he thought one of the lights might have been the moon, but as the authors noted, the moon wasn't full that night. Ms. Fountain was about 10 years old at the time, and even though her father never spoke of the incident again until just before his death in 1991, she never forgot his story. She knew her father as a serious man; making up an occurrence like that just wasn't in his nature. And his ongoing silence about the incident seemed to add weight to his story—it was difficult for him to speak of it, even to his dearest kin.

The idea that two objects might have been involved in the incident that night off the coast near Shag

Harbour was further supported when Ledger and Styles examined the timeline between Wickens' report and another account provided by Norm Smith. Smith had seen an object in the night sky twice that night, but according to his timeline the second sighting occurred while Wickens was watching his flying object sink into the harbour. Apparently the authors ran on a tip and contacted a military officer who might have the information they were looking for. The officer was apparently one of the radio officers on duty with the Royal Canadian Air Force, and although he couldn't break confidentiality and discuss any details, he did say that he believed there were "two objects that went into the water that night."

For a while the events of October 4, 1967, were all anyone could talk about. Then just as suddenly, the strange incident was almost out of bounds. People never forgot that night, but they kept their thoughts to themselves. Although Lawrence Smith played an important role in the initial rescue operation, even his own brother wouldn't discuss what happened that night with him.

Styles and Ledger's years of research into the subject, and the release of *Dark Object*, seemed to infuse the people of Nova Scotia with a renewed interest in what remains an unexplained event. It also gave folks a sense of permission to revisit that night and ponder anew what might have happened. With all the official documents, incident reports and other correspondence surrounding the Shag Harbour Incident now in the public forum, the perceived cone of silence people might have felt was being imposed on them so many years ago had been lifted.

Thanks in part to *Dark Object*, the Shag Harbour story was alive again in the minds of locals. Renewed interest in the unsolved incident also intrigued the general public, and avid ufologists were reminded of the case and revisited it with new energy. Shag Harbour post-mistress Cindy Nickerson was the driving force behind the post office releasing an official stamp on May 18, 2001, commemorating Shag Harbour as the "Home of the '67 UFO Visit." And the Shag Harbour Incident Society Museum (also known by locals as the UFO Museum) was established, and over the years it has continued to grow and remains relevant to the residents of the area and visitors alike.

Perhaps someone out there knows what really happened off the coast of Shag Harbour. Maybe it was a government experiment or a high-tech, top-secret craft out on a simple, training manoeuvre. Possibly it was just a strange atmospheric manifestation. Whatever the answer, the Shag Harbour Incident remains one of the world's most unique UFO incidents in recorded history—and one of Canada's biggest unsolved mysteries.

CHAPTER EIGHT

Newfoundland

DSTI's (Directorate Scientific and Technical Intelligence) *assessment is that the type of rocket depicted in the photographs cannot be determined with the available information. The information that has been determined from an analysis of the photographs was used to rule out several possibilities. The object is not a ballistic missile, not a cruise missile in boost phase nor a cruise missile in flight phase. It is also not a licensed model rocket launch, either.*

–Press Release, Government Operations Centre,
Department of National Defence

Harbour Mille: Mystery on The Rock

A CERTAIN FLAVOUR OF PEOPLE hail from "The Rock." Newfoundland and Labrador's distinguished history of being known as Canada's newest province, having only entered Confederation in 1949, speaks to the strength, resilience and independence of its residents. In Newfoundland and Labrador, you needed those kinds of character traits to live in what can often be an unyielding wilderness.

Throughout the centuries, the rocky, winding shores that are characteristic of this Atlantic seaboard has tried and tested European visitors. Initial attempts to establish a permanent settlement were more often than not unsuccessful; the oldest European village, L'Anse aux Meadows, is thought to have been settled by Leif Erikson's third landing some time around 990 AD. The site was discovered in 1968, and it appears settlers didn't live in L'Anse aux Meadows for very long—one source suggests ongoing occupancy of this settlement lasted until 1050 AD.

It would be another 500 years before John Cabot "rediscovered" Newfoundland, in 1497 (some historians argue it was actually a Portuguese mariner named Joao Fernandes Lavrador who initially charted this corner of our country).

Even the names of communities speak to both the geography and the mindset of the people living there. "Cove," "bay," "brook," "land," "bank," "harbour" and "town" are just a few of the geographic descriptors coupled with a name, an event or an emotion that evokes imaginings of the place's history, its joys, its sorrows. I've always wondered where the name Heart's Desire came from, and how Conception Bay might have gotten its name.

In the southern part of the province, just a stone's throw from the French island of Saint-Pierre and Miquelon, is Fortune Bay. This part of the province was settled around the end of the 18th century, and the name Fortune Bay was certainly a fitting one.

Because fishing was historically one of Newfoundland and Labrador's prime resources, the folks migrating south and nestling into the villages dotting this protected isthmus were in many ways showered with good fortune, indeed. While the rest of the province has struggled in the past years with a depletion of cod stocks, the same is not true for Fortune Bay. Cod stocks here remain stable, and a fisherman can still make a decent living.

Tucked away in the most northeasterly corner of Fortune Bay in the Burin Peninsula is the community of Harbour Mille. Folks here are among those who still rely on fishing to earn their keep. But in recent, years other attractive entrepreneurial options have presented themselves. The explosion of public interest in the ecotourism industry has drawn Canadians and foreign visitors alike to the farthest reaches of this country's boundaries, and Harbour Mille offers endless beauty and a wilderness experience that can rival just about any other.

This small, protected village of about 200 people is a place where humans and nature live in a kind of harmony not often seen in the Western world. Tours put on by businesses like Coastal Safari offer five- and eight-day tours where a person can "live with the rhythm of sun, moon and tides." Participants spend their time kayaking, hiking, fishing and exploring the wilderness around them, and if they're smart, they bring their cameras along for the ride.

Even the residents of Harbour Mille don't take the beauty of their natural environment for granted. It might have been a chilly January day in 2010, but the sunset outside Darlene Stewart's window was too beautiful to ignore. Stopping just long enough to retrieve her camera and pull on a warm coat, Stewart rushed outside and began snapping away.

Now if you've ever seen a sunset off the southern coast of Newfoundland you'll understand why Stewart was so eager to record its beauty. A kaleidoscope of colour illuminates the horizon, which is sometimes dotted with the odd cloud or dimmed slightly by a rising fog. That night, though, the sky was clear and the colours amazing.

Positioning herself to capture as much of the scene as she could, Stewart began snapping photographs. Suddenly, something caught her eye. At first she couldn't really determine what it was. Deciding to zoom in as much as she could, Stewart began taking photos again, this time shooting the strange object in the sky. Clearly it was moving. And it seemed to her as though bright, yellow-orange flames were trailing behind and propelling it forward, resembling what she imagined a rocket would look like.

"Even with the camera, I couldn't make it out," Stewart later told reporters with CBC News. She reasoned that downloading the pictures to her computer would give her a better image of what she was seeing. But she did know one thing for certain: "I knew then it wasn't an airplane. It was something different."

The object was still sailing through the sky when she called over her husband and her neighbour, Emmy Pardy, to see what she'd been watching. Soon, there wasn't just a single object; there were three. "It appeared to come out of the ocean," Pardy told CBC News of one of the additional objects. "It was like it was in the middle of the bay."

Once all three were airborne, one was clearly closer to the trio of observers than the other two and at that point appeared to disappear into the horizon along with the sunset that had originally captivated Stewart. The unidentified flying objects didn't make a sound. The scene unnerved the three witnesses. "I really did get sick to my stomach. I was shaking when I seen it," she said. "We were just in awe of what we seen."

Having witnessed the strange scene with her friend and husband was somewhat comforting: two important people in her life would not only believe her story, but they could also collaborate it. The assortment of photographs Stewart took added some credibility to her tale, especially when she informed the authorities of the sighting.

Whether or not her photographs would be enough to help get to the bottom of this mystery, only time would tell.

Pictures and a collection of witnesses are usually enough to get the RCMP and other officials interested in claims of a strange sighting. But if the authorities needed a push to take Stewart's concerns seriously, there was another sure way to make that happen—by getting the media involved.

The day after the event, CBC News led with the story, "UFO Sighting Puzzles NL Residents." The headline captured the attention of the entire country, but in all honesty, Stewart and her companions weren't worried that what they saw was a UFO in the traditional sense. Rather, they were concerned that military experiments were going on in their area that residents didn't know about, or that perhaps another country might have been doing some unannounced missile testing.

And that's exactly where officials began their investigation—examining the photographs Steward took that night over the Burin Peninsula and querying Canada's military.

According to an official press release from the Department of National Defence and the Directorate Scientific and Technical Intelligence, dated January 28, 2010, the "only missiles that are launched from a submarine are large ballistic missiles or cruise missiles." With Pardy's testimony stating she'd seen at least one of the "rockets" shooting up from the water, checking out if something might have been discharged from a submarine was a logical starting point in the investigation. But no permits had been issued or requested for a missile or rocket launch in the area, so officials turned to the images provided by witnesses.

While other photos may have been snapped that night, Stewart's quick camera action was particularly useful. Some of the images were slightly blurred, but the overall quality of the pictures was fairly clear and focused, and officials were able to examine the strange aerial object in considerable detail.

What they analyzed simply didn't support the theory that the fiery object in the sky might have been a missile. They argued that the flame being expelled from the back end was "atypical of a missile launch." In particular, the "flame tail [did not] exhibit the pointed shape created in supersonic gas flow."

The length of the flame was off, too, as was its colour. Jet engine exhaust from a cruise missile wouldn't be greater in length than the "rocker body." As for the colour, it should have been white: the flames in this case were orange.

Further query confirmed that neither NORAD nor Canada Command (CANCOM)—a branch of the Canadian Forces responsible for national security operations—had noticed anything on their radar to support the sighting.

Because official answers into the investigation were anything but conclusive, CTV News consulted three aerospace experts about what they thought of the photo images and the likelihood that the objects were missiles or something far less dangerous, such as hobby rockets. Again, their opinions were inconclusive.

"This is not an amateur rocket. This is more likely a military missile," Dr. David Greatrix, professor of Aerospace Engineering at Toronto's Ryerson University, told reporters. He went on to suggest that although no official military activity was going on at the time, there was a "very small chance that it was an inadvertent launch."

Dr. Billy Allan, professor at the Royal Military College in Kingston, Ontario, and a former experimental flight test engineer with the DND, disagreed. "There's nothing that travels that fast (the speed of sound) that you can sit there and take pictures of it," he argued, adding the photo could very well be of a "sophisticated model rocket."

Jeremy Laliberte, an assistant professor of Aerospace Engineering at Carleton University, echoed Allan's suggestion. "My first thought was some sort of hobbyist with a home-built thing gone awry, and they may not want to admit it," Laliberte said, adding that these hobby rockets can "remain suspended in air for up to 15 minutes."

Even a Finnish UFO researcher shared his views on what the object in Stewart's photos might have been. Bjorn Borg suggested the photo could have indeed captured the image of a rocket or missile, and that something called the "December Phenomenon" was responsible for the image.

"Every year this comes up in the news," he told Canadian Press reporters from his home in Helsinki. He went on to suggest that "what people are really seeing is the effect of jetliner vapour trails catching winter sunlight....The sun is shining on the (condensation) trail. In wintertime, the colour of the trail will show up (a) very strong yellow or even red. It looks like fire."

Simply put, the photo could have just been a snap of a jetliner.

"I've seen this several times," Chris Stevenson, then-president of St. John's Royal Astronomical Society, told reporters.

Residents of Harbour Mille and the surrounding area knew what they thought about the differing opinions. They were still pondering the possibility that test missiles had been launched by France's military at Saint-Pierre and Miquelon. But the French Ministry of Defence was quick to put an end to that theory. They had indeed launched a test-fire of their M51 ballistic missiles from a submarine the same week as the sightings, but not until January 27, two days after the sighting occurred. They also pointed out that the missile had been launched in the opposite direction of the sightings as described by the witnesses.

By the end of the week, the residents of Harbour Mille, and indeed the rest of the country, were no closer to discovering what the mysterious airborne object was than they had been the night it was reported. The only official comment provided by RCMP sergeant Wayne Edgecombe to CBC News on the matter was, "We confirmed that it was something." But he was not at liberty to disclose exactly what the investigation might have uncovered, other than that it was "nothing criminal."

For several days, media outlets queried the RCMP, the Department of National Defence and Public Safety Canada in an effort to get to the bottom of the mystery, but no further information was forthcoming from any of the three organizations.

Even when Liberal MP Gerry Byrne, from the Newfoundland riding of Humber-St. Barbe-Baie Verte, chimed in and challenged the federal government to come forward with a "straightforward, factual state-ment," no other statements were released. Byrne went on record saying the entire event had been "cloaked in relative secrecy."

Aside from the concern that missile testing was going on and the public was ignorant of the fact, statements like the one issued from the prime minister's office just days after the sighting, suggesting that a hobbyist in the area may have launched a model rocket, raised the ire of Newfoundlanders. Then-minister Peter MacKay's flippant joke that the government would "provide money to build a landing strip for UFOs at Harbour Mille" only added fuel to the public's frustration.

Even Danny Williams, premier of Newfoundland and Labrador at the time, backed the government claims that there was nothing to worry about. Having met with Prime Minister Stephen Harper on January 29, Williams stated that he was "confident Canada (the federal government) was not aware of any missile testing that it was not telling the province about."

"Yeah, right, I don't believe that for one minute," Pardy told Canadian Press reporters in May 2010. "It was no model rocket...You don't even have to be a rocket scientist to figure that one out." Pardy went on to say she believed the government knew what had happened, and they were covering up the truth. "Somebody made a blunder somewhere."

As of this writing, more than a year has passed since that lovely sunset beckoned Darlene Stewart to take its portrait. A year has come and gone since the small village of Harbour Mille was propelled into the public spotlight. A year since a strange object shot overhead, and no one but the residents who lived there seemed to be the least concerned about finding an answer.

Chances are the years will continue to move along and the unusual story will become little more than a family tale handed down from generation to generation.

Whatever the airborne anomaly actually was, it will likely remain listed as another one of this country's strangest unidentified flying objects.

CHAPTER NINE

Northwest Territories

Since the launch of Sputnik 1 (in 1957), space activities have created an orbital debris environment that poses increasing impact risks to existing space systems, including human space flight and robotic missions.

–Nicholas Johnson, American bureaucrat, author and professor

Coppermine: Classified Documents

SMALL COMMUNITIES ARE TYPICALLY tight-knit, and this is especially true the more geographically remote the community. For the more than 1300 residents of Kugluktuk, a hamlet located at the mouth of the Coppermine River in Canada's newest territory of Nunavut, relying on one another in all aspects of life is essential. And any perceived threat to that way of life is aggressively challenged.

Prior to January 1, 1996, Kugluktuk was known as Coppermine, named after the river. Situated in the most northern and barren portion of this country's Canadian Shield, Kugluktuk has its own store, post office, schools and a Hunters and Trappers Association. With a primarily Inuit population, Kugluktuk is a place of history, a place where stories are passed from generation to generation and where the elders are the keepers of an oral tradition that is sacred.

With that in mind, a UFO sighting would definitely rank as an important story to hold on to.

Two men were walking through town at about 1:30 PM on March 18, 1961, when they noticed a strange entity soaring vertically through a clear blue sky, as if a jet was plummeting to the earth and emitting a vapour trail. One of the observers noticed that as the object neared, it looked like it was "twisting or pitching, trailing dark-brown smoke, with blood-red flame in the smoke." It was silver but was definitely unlike any aircraft he'd seen in his life. Suddenly, there were two loud explosions, followed by a plume of smoke, which disappeared after a short time behind the Couper Islands. However, the vapour trail produced during the craft's descent hung in the air for hours. The event was so strange that the men decided to report the sighting.

While the men were watching the trail of smoke writing itself onto the horizon, another witness was enjoying the mild temperatures and walking his dog. He was also intrigued by the vapour trail he was watching develop, so much so that he drew a map of what he estimated was its location, though he didn't report it to the authorities until the following day.

Not far away, a hunter was searching for caribou near the Asiak River when his focus was distracted by the sound of "two reports in quick succession from due north." Two other hunters heard the same thing, though they suggested that from their position, one explosion sounded as if it came from the northwest and the other from a more general northwesterly direction. And another witness heard a single explosion west of his location. None of these individuals reported looking up to the sky or noticing the vapour trails. A woman, however, did report seeing the object in question and echoed many of the same details as the two men who first reported the sighting.

David O'Brien, area administrator with the Coppermine Detachment, took the statements from these and various other witnesses. The information provided to him, if it was indeed accurate, suggested that the object:

...had a functioning engine burning fuel, and that the burning material was not the object incandescing through friction in the tropopause. The description of the smoke and flame at lower altitude does not tally with the usual appearance of smoke and flame issuing from a stricken aircraft burning petroleum based fuel.

O'Brien theorized that the witnesses' claim of two explosions might have suggested the sound of initial impact and the sonic boom resulting from the subsequent shock waves. The individual reporting a single explosion could have experienced the initial impact and subsequent shock wave at the same time. O'Brien further suggested that:

> ...*the object, in order to be visible to the naked eye at a distance of twenty-five miles* [40 kilometres], *must have been unusually large, especially since an axial movement could be observed. An impact (or impact explosion) clearly audible at twenty-five miles would indicate an explosion of sufficient intensity as to create a large crater.*

Reflecting on his past experiences, O'Brien knew that anything hitting the earth at "near-sonic speed" and crashing into the ground would leave a crater that would be about 12 metres deep and 38 metres in diameter. Mathematically, it all made sense. But with the snow still falling, and a few weeks to go before spring arrived at this corner of the country, an aerial search wouldn't be productive.

Officials from the Department of Northern Affairs and National Resources took a slightly different approach to the idea of searching the area. From their perspective, a ground search was imperative, but to accommodate such a search, they needed to secure a dog team. It took two full days to find a dog team capable of traversing the challenging geography, and at 9:15 AM on March 21, Kuliktanna, the Inuit assistant, and an unnamed officer broke through the snow on a clear, cold day, travelling a full nine hours before reaching what they believed might have been the impact area, and the highest elevation around.

The officer, assistant and group of tired dogs set camp for the night. According to the officer:

> *By nightfall, nothing unusual had been observed, and the scanning and search were resumed the following morning with negative results. By mid-morning, the search was abandoned and we started on the return trip.*

At this point, the officer conceded that an aerial search might have been more productive, and the team abandoned its efforts. At the same time, the final report submitted to Mr. Hawrelak of the Department of Transport acknowledged what the RCMP had already determined—that an air search wouldn't accomplish much at that time of year unless the suspected crash impact left a large crater. Wind, snow and winter weather would continue for some time to come, and it was clear that nothing short of a miracle would produce any answers until the milder summer conditions were upon them.

The first report filed on the Coppermine sighting was classified as confidential. It remained so for years, even though the investigation hadn't yielded a reason for that classification.

However, there were hints about the secrecy. Inklings of suspicion from certain individuals in authority pointed to all kinds of possibilities that could stir great imaginings in the minds of conspiracy theorists.

A memorandum from L.C. Dilworth, air commodore for Chief of the Air Staff, RCAF, to the Air Defence Command Headquarters, based in the RCAF station in Saint-Hubert, Québec, dated August 21, 1961, summarized NORAD's assessment of the sighting:

> ...Remote possibility object was small fragment transit 3B or SPUTNIK IX primary bodies of which re-entered 30 Mar and 9–10 Mar respectively. Satellite re-entry normally readily identified from meteorite as display appears to be burning aircraft entering at low angle and is visible for several minutes. Depending on location of observer display may be visible from horizon to horizon. Motion is much slower than normal meteorite impact.

Russia's early expeditions into outer space, known as the Sputnik Program, were a matter of much upheaval for the United States, and by default, Canada. Many of the details surrounding the space program were considered classified information, but the launch of *Sputnik 1* on October 4, 1957, and its successful orbit of the earth was a technological first that propelled Russia to the forefront in space exploration, and it severely bruised the American ego.

At that time, the United States was also working on its own space projects, but early attempts at satellite launches had failed. The success of *Sputnik 1* gave Russia an upper hand, opening the door to a succession of *Sputnik* satellites being launched throughout the years with the goal of collecting various types of data. During the Cold War era, there was no telling what that could mean. Still, even Dilworth admitted that he couldn't provide a logical reason why the original report couldn't be downgraded to unclassified.

It's not clear when the files on the Coppermine sightings were finally unclassified, but they were among the thousands of documents released to Library and Archives Canada when Prime Minister Stephen Harper opened files to the public between 2005 and 2009.

Any concrete explanation about what people saw on that brisk spring day was not forthcoming. The object that whizzed across the sky and slammed into the landscape, leaving behind it a trail of smoke and flames was never identified. But it's a story that, like the historic legends of the people who call that region home, will remain a part of the Inuit oral tradition for many generations to come.

Part Three

ALIENS AMONG US

CHAPTER TEN

Sacred Geometry or Spurious Hoax?

Crop circles have had a profound effect on thousands of people who have witnessed and studied them through the years. Irrespective of origin, they have acted as a catalyst to learning, understanding and spirituality as we strive to understand the meaning and purpose behind the genuine crop circles.

–Paul Vijay, CropCircleResearch.com

Crop Circle Overview

THE OVERNIGHT APPEARANCE of intricate patterns super-imposed in a farmer's field isn't a new phenomenon. Reports of the strange occurrence we usually call crop circles, but which are also known as agriglyphs or crop formations because not all of the geometric patterns are circles, first appeared in written texts as far back as the 17th century. For years the appearance of these formations has stumped residents living in their vicinity; it is a conundrum most farmers want an answer to, and they want the occurrences to stop. The last thing farmers need as their ripened fields of wheat, barley and other grains near harvest time is to have someone or something flattening their crops.

Putting the logical concerns aside, the intricacies of some of these field images are astounding. Some of them flow so perfectly and are so detailed—like the 238-metre diameter crop circle described as a "six-sided triskelion composed of 409 circles" that popped up in a field in Milk Hill, England—that they completely defy explanation. If they are indeed created by humans, what method can produce such a perfect picture in such a short time without leaving any evidence as to how the design was created or the identity of the artist?

Of course this line of thinking leads us to the consideration that these pieces of art might not be the work of two-legged creatures. Perhaps they are created by nature, and strange weather patterns or some type of meteorological phenomena are responsible. After all, nature's splendour offers the most magnificent beauty the world has to offer.

In 1880, an investigator named John Rand Capron posited the theory that a rash of particularly violent storms in Western Surrey might have been responsible for the strange patterns that had been appearing in some of the wheat fields in the area. After he had expended considerable time investigating the fields where these storms had occurred, his findings, along with a plea to readers to come forward with their stories if they witnessed something similar, were printed in the July 29, 1880, edition of *Nature* magazine. Capron explained that he and his neighbour found sections of his neighbour's wheat field had been levelled "in patches forming, as viewed from a distance, circular spots." Capron further noticed that the stocks were evenly arranged and generally undamaged:

...The soil is a sandy loam upon the greensand, and the crop is vigorous, with strong stems, and I could not trace locally any circumstances accounting for the peculiar forms of the patches in the field, nor indicating whether it was wind or rain, or both combined, which had caused them, beyond the general evidence everywhere of heavy rainfall. They were suggestive to me of some cyclonic wind action, and may perhaps have been noticed elsewhere by some of your readers.

That weather is responsible for some of these patterns is perhaps something observers can vouch for first-hand. Urban legends of farmers witnessing a crop circle being formed can be found on every continent: some might suggest that a person must simply be in the right place at the right time. On his website, David Pratt recounts one story of how a farmer and his son watched as a sudden, furious wind happened upon them, centring its attention on a segment of the farmer's field and forming a crop circle in scant seconds in Essex, England, in 1931. The farmer called the sight a "Devil's twist," which was a term used since the 1830s to explain that kind of occurrence.

In another account, Pratt tells of a woman who, in 1934, was "gazing over a field of corn when she heard a fire-like crackling sound and saw a whirlwind in the centre of the field, spinning stalks, seeds and

dust up into the air for about 100 feet [30 metres]."
When the wind stopped, the woman, whose exact
geographic location wasn't mentioned, walked over
to the field and noticed the corn was "hot to the
touch" and "the plant stalks [had been] interlaced or
even plaited."

If indeed these accounts, and others like them, are
true, it certainly supports the theory that atmospheric
conditions aid in the making of agriglyphs. Still,
even the most dedicated scientist would find it hard to
argue that Mother Nature is completely responsible
for these creations.

It is equally difficult to believe that all of these
patterns are created by people, even after retired
friends Doug Bower and Dave Chorley went public
saying they'd been creating hundreds of these crop
circles between 1977 and 1991 throughout the UK
and later in Queensland, Australia. Several sources
explained how the pair used little more than
"a plank of wood, rope and a baseball cap fitted with
a loop of wire to help them walk in a straight line."
And during some interviews, Bower and Chorley
even demonstrated how they could whip up a crop
circle in no time.

Despite the fact that Chorley and Bower admitted
their scam, many diehard UFO and crop circle
researchers have stated that the men's antics couldn't
account for every discovery. They argued that crop
circles appeared in several places around the world
and not just in England, and that many of those

cases couldn't be explained away using Chorley and Bower's methods or any other technique.

It is logical to suggest that weather might be responsible for some of these geometric patterns, and good-natured hoaxers like Bower and Chorley might be responsible for others. But a significant number of agriglyphs defy either explanation. It is these circles that ufologists and paranormal investigators are most interested in. The circles might provide a key to the age-old question: are we really alone in this big universe?

Duhamel, Alberta: I Do Not Believe!

I'm not at liberty to discuss the government's knowledge of extraterrestrial UFOs at this time. I am still personally being briefed on the subject!

−Richard M. Nixon, former U.S. president

Like most farmers, Edgar Schielke had a system. From the time he got out of bed in the morning to the moment he retired for the night, his day was organized. Chores were completed in an orderly fashion and, for the most part, each day passed without too many big surprises. A system spells success in just about any aspect of life, and this is especially true for farmers who usually juggle countless tasks without a lot of help.

With that in mind, it's important for farmers to instill some kind of routine in their livestock. Training animals to leave for pasture and return home at certain times of the day reduces the amount of energy a farmer has to expend by directing them from place to place. Being a man with a system, Schielke made darned sure his cows knew what he expected of them. So when the herd of cattle belonging to the Duhamel, Alberta, farmer didn't make their nightly trip back to the farm from the pasture on Friday, August 4, 1967, Schielke was a little put out.

It had been raining heavily throughout the day, and perhaps this muddled with his cows' typical routine. Schielke wasn't too keen on going out in the rain to round them up, so he decided to wait until morning. But when they still hadn't come home the next day, he had no choice but to ride out to pasture and collect his brood.

It was the first time in a week or more that Schielke had visited that pasture, and when he arrived, he was a little surprised by what he saw. It looked like someone had made four circular impressions on his land. He wasn't happy that a trespasser visited his property, but he didn't give it much thought, either. It wasn't as if whoever made the markings actually damaged his fencing or a crop or something that would cost him money. What would be the point of reporting the find to the police when there wasn't anything they could do? Making his discovery public would only draw unwanted attention to Schielke's farm without bringing in anything by way of financial compensation. And so he let sleeping dogs lie, as they say—at least that was his intention until he casually mentioned the weird shapes to his neighbour, a teacher by the name of Ray Saunders.

There had been a lot of strange things going on around Duhamel and the surrounding farmland southwest of Camrose. For several weeks leading up to Schielke's find, reports had been trickling into the RCMP about odd sightings and other strange phenomena. And not all complaints were reported; many were just circulated by word of mouth. But in one case, a Captain G. Walker from the Royal Canadian Army Service Corps (RCASC) in Edmonton was called in to interview two young girls who said they'd seen a "largish, creamish" object that looked like a big dish "bobbing up and down near the ground as if to attract attention." According to their statement, the girls were about 200 or 300 yards (180 or 275 metres) away from the sighting at the time. The report was not investigated further.

Of course stories travel, especially in small towns. Saunders, who was a bit of a UFO buff, followed these tales with great interest. After hearing about the patterns on Schielke's field, Saunders took it upon himself to visit the *Camrose Canadian* newspaper and speak with a reporter named Mr. Patridge. Saunders thought the general public should know about the circles, so he told the reporter. Patridge hiked over to the site to check them out for himself, and a story appeared in the pages of the local paper.

Interest was being generated without a whole lot of effort, and it's unclear if Saunders or Schielke eventually contacted the authorities, or if officials followed up on the news article and contacted Schielke. Either way, Captain Walker of the 1 Transport Helicopter Platoon Detachment CFB Edmonton was assigned the task of investigating the markings and liaising with a "scientific officer" from the Defence Research Establishment Experimental Station (DRES) in Suffield.

Although Schielke had no interest in spending the time required to get to the bottom of what caused the mysterious markings in his pasture, he found himself in the middle of a full-scale investigation. But he was adamant about a few things from the very beginning. He firmly stated that he did not believe in UFOs. He was certain that the marks could not have been created by any of his farm equipment. He also had a theory about the most probable cause of the crop circles: he believed that a "strange lightning phenomenon" made the markings. Had he not opened his mouth and told Saunders about the circles, Schielke wouldn't have had to waste his time on such a foolish investigation.

Dr. G.H. Jones boarded an RCAF Otter aircraft shortly after noon on Friday, August 11, and prepared to depart from the DRES, which was located in the southern Alberta village of Ralston. Because of the Department of National Defence's investigations in Manitoba, with regard to the Falcon Lake Incident and the radioactive soil samples uncovered there, it was "deemed advisable" to organize the collection of soil samples at the Duhamel site for comparison purposes— just in case.

A flight to the Camrose area was considerably preferable to the long drive and three-day time commitment Jones' investigation would have otherwise required to travel between Ralston and the central Alberta community where he was headed. It took two hours of planning and a number of "expensive phone calls" before officials finally managed to arrange Jones' transportation. It wasn't all a loss, though. The time had given Jones a chance to discuss his new investigation with his colleagues at the DRES, as well as obtain any additional information on the case from Captain Walker.

Jones finally landed at the Camrose airstrip at 3:30 that afternoon, where he was met by Captain Walker, Walker's son and an army photographer. The group wasted no time in picking up Patridge at the offices of the *Camrose Canadian* and making their way out to Schielke's pasture.

Apparently there were a lot of other folks who wasted no time in checking things out at the Schielke farm, either. The seven days between the time the markings were first noticed and the afternoon Jones arrived had resulted a shocking amount of damage to the site. For one thing, it had rained quite heavily earlier in the week, which obviously wasn't something anyone could do anything about. But the crowds of curious residents who had visited the site hadn't just parked their cars and wandered about on foot; they'd driven onto the pasture, imprinting their tire treads all over the place and in every direction imaginable. Jones and his colleagues were distressed by their findings, but Schielke didn't appear at all fazed.

Schielke's inattentiveness toward the investigation remained a disturbing puzzle for investigators. His complete disinterest seemed to reinforce his belief that nothing other than the weather was to blame for the strange markings in his field and that everyone was wasting their time. But was that all just a ruse? Was it possible Schielke created the circles himself and was just acting a part to deflect any attention away from himself? And if he had, what could he possibly gain by that kind of notoriety? It didn't make sense that a vocal skeptic would create this gong show of an investigation to garner support for the existence of UFOs, and if he had, it didn't seem likely that he would have let the general population trample through the site in question and damage any potential evidence.

Yes, Schielke was almost as big a mystery as the crop circles in his pasture. Still, Jones wasn't about to learn anything by fixating on the farmer. He needed to focus on securing any potential evidence that might have survived the crowds and tire tracks. Surprisingly, Jones found that what he called "the reputed UFO landing marks" were still "quite clearly impressed on the ground" despite the traffic. At first the marks left him disappointed. Why would his superiors go through all the trouble to send him to Duhamel for this, he wondered? But the closer he inspected the scene, the actual markings and the condition of the vegetation, the more Jones realized that there might be more of a puzzle to this situation than he had first thought.

Patridge had already taken measurements at the pasture shortly after the circles were discovered, but Jones took measurements for himself just to be sure. The smallest circular mark measured 9.5 metres in diameter. The largest of the four markings was a little lopsided, or "slightly elliptical," as Jones described it. The imperfection of this circle meant the measurements varied slightly, from 10 metres to 11 metres. As Jones looked at this larger marking, he thought it almost seemed like something that was created by "a very heavily laden wheel with rubber tyre [moving] in an almost complete and accurate circle."

Jones also noted that each of the circles was only about three-quarters complete, as though there was more pressure on the outsides of the three circles than there had been on the inside, leaving a significantly lighter or non-existent impression on those inner edges. There was no evidence that any kind of machinery had rolled up there—no tire tracks obviously belonged to the markings. Jones found it strange that wherever there was a deposit of cow dung, it was "compressed," and yet no tire had rolled over it. The others attending the scene with Jones had the opportunity to view it earlier, and they told Jones that days earlier there had been evidence of treads or lugs or something with "similar protrusions on about a 3-inch [7.5-centimetre] repeating pattern." Simply put, the flattened areas looked as though they had been created by some kind of rolling motion. According to Jones:

> *My main reason for this impression is that although there was some slight variation in the ground level, the high points were no more compressed than were the low points. Nevertheless, one must bear in mind that a week had passed since the marks were made, and this would give some time for recovery of the ground which could confuse this type of evidence.*

Jones went on to explain that the circular markings were uninterrupted by any other indentations either inside or outside of the circle. There was "no exhaust blast, no scorching, no disturbance of the loose surface material." There was also no perceived damage to any of the trees in the area or other surrounding vegetation.

Jones did notice that there were areas where someone had obviously already taken a soil sample, and he was pretty sure it was either Saunders or a member of the UFO society in Edmonton that he belonged to. Saunders was one of those enthusiastic ufologists that could get carried away, and in many ways he'd already done just that; by that point the teacher-turned-investigator had not only spread the word of the strange occurrence to his special interest group and the local media, but he had also contacted the national media about the crop circles, and the CBC was now filing a report on the anomaly.

From what Jones could determine, the circular impressions were vastly different from any tire tracks left during the week since Schielke first noticed the crop circles. They were uniform in appearance and made a deep indentation in the ground. Jones took radiation counts at several different positions in the pasture and although the readings varied between a low of 50 to a high of 200 counts per minute (cpm), they all fell nicely in what he referred to as the normal range.

Jones' investigation wouldn't have much merit if he didn't attempt to critically analyze the possibility of a hoax. He had to at least try to determine if the previous appearance of similar-looking crop circles or UFO sightings in the area was tied in any way to this recent anomaly. Could someone unknown to Schielke be perpetrating hoaxes in the area and trying to make him look guilty? Was Schielke really just a man who had more important things on his mind than some silly flat spots on the ground and couldn't be bothered to pay any attention to what was going on in the investigation? There were any number of reasons that could explain the farmer's dissociative behaviour, but Jones couldn't pin his bets on any one in particular.

He also couldn't prove that the strange markings were the result of a hoax. Jones wrote in his report:

I believe such a track could be produced by a deliberate hoax, but the hoaxers would require some equipment and a great deal of determination. It would be fair to say that if the mark was produced by rolling contact (a wheel), the load on the wheel even allowing for the rain on Friday would require to be at least three times the load on a truck wheel. If the track was produced when the ground was very soft after the rain, I do not see how the hoaxers could have produced these marks in isolation, without leaving some evidence of their approach to the area and departure from it.

Simply put, the weight required to do the job would have equalled about three quarters of a ton moving in a "virtually exact circle," as it was explained in the document. Jones had several ideas about how that could be accommodated. But he had to admit that while those ideas might work, it was highly unlikely they would provide a concrete explanation for the circles. The equipment needed, the environmental conditions and the lack of any physical evidence left behind while creating the scene made the idea of someone perpetrating a hoax highly unlikely.

As if the circles weren't strange enough, Jones' explanation of an otherworldly cause for those circles was even stranger. The "UFO possibility," as he labelled this theory, looked at the idea that it was possible "something [had come] vertically down onto a relatively narrow ring support, either metal, or, a faint possibility, a flexible skirt." In his calculations, Jones estimated that the amount of pressure needed to have produced the marks would have had to be about 30 kilograms per square inch (psi). Using the measurements as he calculated them, Jones estimated the weight required for a load to make that kind of impression was between 100 and 200 tons: Jones points out that such a weight would be "in the right ball park for a large aircraft, or presumably, a small space ship."

There was another significant factor to consider when tossing about the idea of otherworldly involvement. The cattle were acting strange—very strange. It's not that they were acting up or getting sick or anything. They just didn't appear to want to venture anywhere near the markings; according to investigators, "no significant cattle tracks [were] being left."

With just a few short hours on a Friday afternoon to conduct his investigation, Jones gathered what information he could and ended his report with the following conclusions. He noted there was evidence of "strange phenomena" around that neck of the woods prior to this event. He explained that the prior sightings could suggest someone was conniving enough to use them as a "lead-in to a hoax," with the crowning achievement being the circles found on Schielke's farm. However, he was quick to point out that he had no evidence to support that fact. In his final analysis, even Jones had to admit the entire situation could be genuine.

"The marks were sufficiently unique in my experience for me to state categorically that if I saw similar marks elsewhere my tendency to treat the matter as a hoax would be sharply reduced," Jones wrote in his conclusion. "I have not, however, heard of similar markings in any previously reputed UFO landings."

Jones closed by suggesting the "competent authorities" compare the recently discovered markings with those of past investigations to see if anything similar had been observed elsewhere. If physical markings mirroring those found in Duhamel were discovered, it would lend a great deal of credibility to the current investigation. And it could uphold the theory that people like Saunders so fiercely supported—that there are indeed other intelligent life forms in this universe, and they have visited us.

Results from the soil samples were eventually forwarded to investigators. They were negative for radiation. Because there wasn't anything concrete to base any further investigation on, the phenomena of the Duhamel crop circles remained as big a mystery as ever.

Vanderhoof, BC:
Here, There and Everywhere

Regional stories don't always migrate beyond their provincial borders, so it's not all that strange if folks in BC hadn't ever heard of the Duhamel circles, or of crop circles appearing anywhere else in Canada for that matter. What happened in BC, however, wasn't something most people would push aside without at least a little attention—especially if they experienced it first-hand.

Brent Miskuski had an aerial view of the landscape surrounding his hometown when he spotted crop circles in a farmer's field about 5 kilometres east of the Vanderhoof airport on September 6, 2001. The owner and pilot of Central Air Corp. was flying between Prince George and Vanderhoof, a small community about 100 kilometres west, when he noticed the six circles that looked like they'd been "combed into the field" in such a way that they resembled an outline of Mickey Mouse's head.

Miskuski wasted no time in contacting Chad Deetken about his find. Miskuski and Deetken, a crop circle specialist, had met before—three years earlier, when from the vantage point of his plane Miskuski had discovered another set of strange markings in another field. "It just appeared," Miskuski told Gordon Hoekstra of the *Prince George Citizen* of the newest markings. "It's like they were stamped out, just like last time...it's pretty bizarre." Deetken investigated Miskuski's first find and the pilot was hoping Deetken would be interested in checking this one out as well.

The recent scenario felt a lot like déjà vu. Miskuski's first sighting, in 1998, also took place in the golden month of September. Miskuski and pilot Larry Frey were flying over the area in question on the first of that month when they noticed "10 precise circles of varying sizes between 10 to 100 feet wide (3 to 30 metres) in a ripe oat field just beyond the approach to the [Vanderhoof] runway." In that scenario, the oat samples Deetken collected and tested provided an astonishing find: the oats had experienced some cellular changes. Although that didn't explain what caused the markings, it did rule out the likelihood of a hoax.

In the 1998 case, the oats weren't trampled. Instead, it looked like they'd been bent over, with each of the stalks falling over the other in a symmetrical, spiral fashion. Miskuski noted the 2001 circles looked the same, at least from his vantage point. But there were differences, too. For one thing, they had appeared in a barley field, and there were fewer of them, and they had a rougher quality to them. "I don't think these ones are as nice as the first ones," he told reporters from the *Omineca Express.*

For Brian Vike, a UFO researcher from Houston, BC, his first glimpse of the circles was exciting on two fronts. He was an avid ufologist with an interest in all manner of strange phenomena, so the markings gave him a mystery to study. As well, Vike admitted the circles discovered near Vanderhoof were the first he'd ever seen: it was Vike who described the circles as "Mickey Mouse's head."

According to Vike's measurements, the largest circle was "30 feet across [9 metres] and...flattened in a clockwise spiral. The smaller two are 16 and 17 feet [4.8 and 5.2 metres] across, the smaller one flattened in a counter-clockwise spiral and the other clockwise. About 30 feet [9 metres] away lies another 17-foot [5.2-metre] circle in a counter-clockwise pattern. Forty feet [12 metres] from that is a formation of two circles—one is 27-feet 9-inches [8.5 metres] across in a clockwise spiral and the other 19-feet 10-inches [5.8 metres] in a counter-clockwise spiral."

Further, Vike vouched for the fact that aside from his investigation, including his collection of soil and grain samples, no one else had disturbed the site. None of the stalks were damaged, and the spirals tightened the closer they got to the centre. And when he interviewed residents in the area, Vike learned there had been a smoky smell in the air that was so strong one resident had to close her bedroom window "to keep the unpleasant odour out where it belonged." That woman's story was collaborated by at least three other witnesses, and though Vike couldn't prove the smell had any connection with the appearance of the circles, it was curious. It was doubly curious that the witnesses talking about the smell hadn't heard about the crop circles in their midst.

Although Vike and other investigators who later visited the site left with their samples and prepared to have them analyzed for radiation or other indications that they might have experienced some kind of chemical alteration, official results on those findings were never released. It was another story that basically died in the media, and as soon as the newspapers, radio stations and television newscasts lost interest, it seemed like everyone else did, too.

For some of the folks living in the area, the unexplained crop circles appearing over the years have taken on a larger-than-life status. Many of the residents identify with these stories beyond a superficial level—it's something that in many ways defines who they are. And as long as this current generation exists, the stories of these crop circles will remain a central focus of coffee room chatter and fodder for the legends that will persist for years to come.

CHAPTER ELEVEN

Livestock Beware!

*Six years ago, when the chamber got a call asking if
they knew someone who could check out an animal,
I went thinking no way. It wasn't killed by aliens.
Now, well, I'm not going to come right out and say
there are UFOs. But like a lot of people in town, I am
a little more accepting of strange phenomena.*

–Fernand Belzil, cattle-mutilation expert,
St. Paul, Alberta

St. Paul, Alberta: One-of-a-Kind Expert Investigator

ANIMAL MUTILATION IS CONSIDERED a fairly recent occurrence. Some sources suggest accounts of this bizarre and barbaric occurrence have been reported as far back as the late 19th- and early 20th-century England, but the first reports in the U.S. date back to Alamosa, Colorado, in 1967. In that case, a three-year-old horse named Lady (mistakenly named Snippy by the media) was discovered strangely butchered. All that was left of her head and neck were bones, the cuts involved in the butchering were clean, and the scene was free of blood but had a lingering medicinal odour.

Because of the extraordinary qualities of these kinds of stories, which depict scenes that even the most jaded police officer couldn't push out of his mind, it's just easier to blame whatever committed such an atrocity on an alien life form.

However, animal butchery isn't unique to England and the U.S.

It isn't clear when a similar case was reported in Canada for the first time, but if there's something everyone agrees on, it's that Canada has one key man to turn to when a case of animal mutilation occurs, and that man is Fernand Belzil.

A retired cattle farmer from the St. Paul area, Belzil is considered a one-of-a-kind expert in Canada in a specialty that most folks don't even know about, much less discuss. Belzil deals with the somewhat gruesome task of determining what might have been responsible for the bizarre killing and mutilation of farm animals, which most often involves cattle, in Alberta, Saskatchewan and throughout North America.

Belzil's unique expertise has gained him a considerable amount of notoriety. Not only is he known in the world of unidentified and unexplained phenomena as a specialist in the field, but stories also have been written about him in local and regional media, and he was the focus of a feature story in *Maclean's* magazine.

Belzil says what he sees when he's called out to investigate a strange animal death is often a replica of what he has witnessed in earlier cases. The dead animal is usually the result of what most folks would consider a "clean kill," meaning the carcass wasn't ripped apart by a predator. The animal's blood is often drained. Organs have been surgically removed or the carcass has undergone some other strange procedure. And there's a lack of evidence at the scene pointing to what might have happened.

The town of St. Paul has a UFO hotline welcoming calls on "UFO sightings, cattle mutilations, abductions, crop circles and encounters of all kinds," and with an invitation like that, you're got to have someone in your back pocket to call on in the case of an emergency. That's where Belzil comes in.

The seasoned farmer checked out his first dead cow in the mid-1990s after the local Chamber of Commerce received a call asking for help. Since then he has investigated dozens of animal deaths that he couldn't explain. In 2001 he told reporters from *Maclean's* that there are times when he has been asked to view a cattle mutilation and it's been as if "the body [was] dropped from the sky."

Belzil attends a new case without the kind of bias that some might bring to the scene, but by this point in his career, he's not quite the skeptic he used to be. "I [used to go] thinking no way...it wasn't killed by aliens," he told *Maclean's*. "Now, well, I'm not going to come right out and say there are UFOs. But like a lot of people in town, I am a little more accepting of the strange phenomena."

Belzil's perspective on animal mutilations has evolved from thinking most cases were a result of wild animals desperate for a meal to begrudgingly accepting there might be something unexplained going on: there were just too many situations he couldn't explain. "Ears [that] are removed, circular patches of skin taken off the stomach and face, unexplained bare spots on an animal's body, rectal areas [that] are defiled and…never any blood around." These kinds of images have left most experts speechless, and Belzil is no exception.

What or who may be mutilating animals sporadically across this country, and why anyone would want to do such a thing, is unknown; the killings have been alternately blamed on heartless villains and beings from another planet.

In the meantime, should anyone ever prove the existence of UFOs, and should these alien beings ever want to make contact with humankind, there is a nice landing pad in northeastern Alberta that's waiting to accommodate their arrival.

CHAPTER TWELVE

Alien Abductions

It was real. [Aliens] were plugged into me. It was a download situation. This was long before computers or any kind of wireless... Looking back now, it was like, "F***, they downloaded something into me" Or they uploaded something from my brain, like an experiment.

–Sammy Hagar, former band member of
the group Van Halen, from his memoir,
Red: My Uncensored Life in Rock

Up Close and Personal

IF YOU THINK THE SUBJECT of alien abduction is something that's relegated to episodes of the *Twilight Zone* and *X-Files*, think again. Hundreds of people have professed to being abducted by aliens, and they aren't all celebrities and don't all live south of the border. That said, the case of the Reed family and Betty and Barney Hill probably raised the profile of alien abductions.

The Reed family is a unique case—more unique than most alien abduction claims, that is.

In 1954 Angie Reed told her mother Nancy about an abduction she'd experienced. Angie no doubt believed her story would shock her mother, but the young woman's news wasn't as surprising as her mother's response.

Nancy told Angie of an abduction she believed she experienced as a young child, and so began America's most extraordinary tales of multi-generational abductions that involved several family members and occurred over decades.

The story shared by Betty and Barney Hill was probably one of America's most sensational abduction stories. The couple claimed they were abducted and held hostage on September 19 and 20, 1961, and in 1966 their story eventually made its way into a best-selling book entitled *The Interrupted Journey*, and the subsequent made-for-TV movie *The UFO Incident* in 1975.

Here in Canada, the subject of alien abductions isn't a new topic, but it's met with considerably greater skepticism and, one might argue, a lot less media fanfare than similar situations in the U.S.

On September 3, 1995, the *Vancouver Province* reported that as many as 180 people in the Vancouver area alone believe they'd been abducted by aliens. Although not all of these claims are credible, about 50 of them warranted a deeper investigation according to Mike Strainic of the Mutual UFO Network (MUFON), an American non-profit organization founded on May 30, 1969.

Strainic directed reporters to a woman identified only as "Cindy" as an example. A single woman in her 30s, Cindy agreed to speak with *Vancouver Province* reporters only by phone to ensure her identity remained anonymous. With that safeguard in place, she shared how she'd endured night terrors about being visited by "creatures" on a nightly basis, and how she'd wake up with "fingerprint-sized bruises all over her body." She saw the creatures that attacked her—tall, gangly bipeds with large heads.

When someone finally suggested that maybe Cindy's experiences were alien encounters, the fear of the unknown was somewhat removed, and she felt liberated in knowing others in Canada had experienced something similar. Still, she wasn't about to go public with her story.

Thirty-nine-year-old Arva Abraham wasn't worried about the public knowing her name. She spoke to Kevin Gillies of the *Abbotsford Times* about how she'd been visited regularly by grey-coloured aliens "with large heads, long narrow eyes, and long three fingered hands." She said she'd woken with "vague memories of aliens probing and inspecting her with medical tools and lasers," and she'd find burns and scars on her body.

Former Simon Fraser University psychologist Dr. Barry Beyerstein told Gillies that he believed what

Abraham was really experiencing was a "regular sleep-dream" pattern she was trying to interpret. "In the past, similar experiences were attributed to demons, fairies or witches," he said. "There's a lot of people out there who fervently believe it."

Repeated abductions don't seem to be that uncommon; it appears that individuals don't even report an abduction until they've experienced multiple abductions. The topic of alien abductions in this country even made it on the late radio host Peter Gzowski's "Morningside."

On October 8, 1986, the talk-show host welcomed a woman going by the alias of "Charlotte Brown." She reported being abducted by "4-foot-6-inch (1.5-metre) extraterrestrials" at the age of nine, and then again when she was 15. According to Charlotte, the aliens "inserted a needle-like probe into her abdomen and a burr-shaped tracking device up her nostril."

A 48-year-old Surrey artist only going by the name of Dana would have discounted Beyerstein's repeated-dream theory. Her experience was far too real for her liking. Despite the popular notion that artists are typically high-strung and prone to emotional mood swings, Dana's partner told *Vancouver Sun* reporter Mia Stainsby that Dana was "level-headed" and kept him "from becoming overly analytical about life." And yet Dana said aliens have abducted her several times.

Dana believes her first abduction took place when she was in her late 20s. She remembers that experience vividly. She was trying to get to sleep when the commonly described grey alien swept her away from her bed and into its aircraft. She remembers four other women and two men being put into "capsules" and transported to a "mother ship."

Once on the ship, Dana's story becomes even more frightening. She felt paralyzed, and at some point the creatures must have stopped her heart from beating because she remembered being "jolted back to life from what felt like being frozen dead."

Dana's second abduction a few years later was more vague. In any case, the experiences left her scarred and plagued by nightmares. It wasn't until she learned about the Mutual UFO Network and discovered she wasn't the only person to have had this kind of experience that she became convinced her experience was real and not a hallucination.

She went through hypnosis and shared her experience with other abductees, and though Dana remains reluctant to go public and let the media identify her, she is at peace in the knowledge that what she experienced was real.

In 2002, Krista Henriksen acquired her MA in anthropology from Simon Fraser University with her thesis *Alien Encounters: A Close Analysis of Personal Accounts of Extraterrestrial Experiences*. A member of the

United Church of Canada, and a student of sociology and anthropology, Henriksen examined the topic from the perspective of studying belief systems, as well as learning what motivates people.

After analyzing 60 accounts provided by both men and women, Henriksen isolated four themes that ran through the stories:

The first is that the person receiving the message is in some way chosen or special—they have a purpose in life. Second is the message that that person is not alone; someone cares for them. Third is the idea that the world is at risk, but the recipient has the power to affect change. And finally, there are few aliens who bring malevolent messages, but they are definitely in the minority.

After assessing her findings, Henriksen came to the conclusion that the "whole phenomenon is a direct reflection of the search for meaning in the world," not unlike the "correspondent explosion in new religious movements in North America."

Although Henriksen's research is as unbiased as possible, not everyone would agree with her conclusion. For those individuals who believe they'd been swept away against their will and their bodies were used as guinea pigs, no amount of debate is going to change their minds.

CHAPTER THIRTEEN

Conclusion

...The appearance of the wheels and their workings was like the colour of beryl, and all four had the same likeness. The appearance of their workings was, as it were, a wheel in the middle of a wheel. When they moved, they went toward any one of four directions; they did not turn aside when they went. As for their rims, they were so high they were awesome; and their rims were full of eyes, all around the four of them. When the living creatures went, the wheels went beside them; and when the living creatures were lifted up from the earth, the wheels were lifted up...

–Ezekiel 1:16–19

A Final Word

CYLINDRICAL OBJECTS. Rows of flickering lights. Wheel-shaped objects rotating in the sky. A crescent-shaped entity glowing in the dark night. Human-like beings with oddly shaped heads. Spiral patterns similar to those on a snail's shell.

Stories about strange sightings and unexplained encounters such as those mentioned in this book have been a part of human history time immemorial.

We could presume it was the allure of the night sky and its show of shooting stars and the meteorites exploding every now and again that propelled the human mind into otherworldly wonderings. Or perhaps it was the visual trickery of a full moon or an eclipse that thrust prehistoric minds into a world of unknown imaginings.

But the intricate details of the world's first cave paintings, which chronicle unexplainable scenes that appear to include saucer-shaped spacecraft—clearly not a technology the artists etching those images onto rock would have been familiar with—would leave that kind of hypothesis in doubt. A leap of imagination that far outside the realm of our current experience just doesn't seem likely.

So what are we to make of these objects of art depicting some kind of unexplained encounter? What about the cave paintings, or ancient sculptures like the stone carvings discovered in Iraq that date to between 5000 and 4500 BC? What about the painting frantically etched into a drawer bottom so that what-ever the creator experienced was documented for all time but was hidden from public view, protecting the artist from the deluge of humiliation that would surely follow its discovery? What do we make of the prophet Ezekiel's experience of seeing suspended in the air a wheel within a wheel with its rims lined with eyes, or other references to strange encounters in other holy scriptures? What does it mean when a fresco located in a church in Arezzo, Italy, includes two saucer-shaped objects hovering in the sky?

Can these representations be reasoned away with scientific explanation? Are the spherical objects in that Italian fresco simply the "stationary lens-shaped clouds that form at high altitudes, normally aligned at right-angles to the wind direction" known as lenticular clouds—one theory proposed by scientists and ufologists throughout the years. Are there some other pneumatic anomalies responsible for these and other sightings? Or do we have company in this universe we call our own? Only time will tell.

Notes on Sources

Media Sources

Archaeology Daily News

CBC News

CTV News

The Discovery Channel

Edmonton Journal

The History Channel

National Post

Prince George Citizen

Omenica Express

Wikipedia

Book Source

Campaga, Palmiro. *The UFO Files: The Canadian Connection Exposed.*
Toronto, Ontario: Dundurn Press. 2010.

Government Sources and Internet Sites

Canada's UFOs: The Search for the Unknown, Library and
Archives Canada, www.collectionscanada.gc.ca

Canadian Nuclear Safety Commission, http://nuclearsafety.gc.ca/
eng/readingroom/factsheets/devices/index.cfm

Department of Defence Canada

RCMP

Shirley's Bay Review, www.canadaconnects.ca/space/main/

UFO Groups and Other Special Interest Websites

"The Vike Factor: Into the Paranormal," http://hbccuforesearch.
blogspot.com/

Alberta UFO Study Group, http://aufosg.com/

Brian Vike, www.rense.com/general28/around.htm

Brian Vike's new website, www.sightings.com/

Chris Rutkowski's UFO Survey, 1990, www.canadianuforeport.
    com/survey/data/90survey.html

HBCCUFO Research, Unidentified Aerial Phenomena Reporting
    Vault, www.hbccufo.org/

Hertzberg Institute of Astrophysics, www.nrc-cnrc.gc.ca/eng/
    ibp/hia.html

Mysteries of Canada: Wilbert Smith, www.mysteriesofcanada.
    com/Canada/project_magnet.htm

Obituary, Stefan Michalak, www.ufoinfo.com/news/michalak.shtml

Rosewell, New Mexico, www.roswellproof.com/index.html

UFO surveys in Canada, www.canadianuforeport.com/survey/essays

www.appalachianghostwalks.com/arc-alternate-realities-center.html

www.usufocenter.com

PSICAN—Paranormal Studies & Investigations Canada,
    www.psican.org/alpha/index.php?/20090217213/Ufological-
Information/Canada-s-X-Files.html

John Rand Capron from the site Normandy Historians, http://
    normandyhistorians.co.uk/capron.html

Winnipeg Realtors, www.winnipegrealtors.ca/editorials.aspx?id=569

The 1967 Shag Harbour UFO Crash, www.roswellproof.com/
    Shag_Harbour/Shag_Harbour1_summary.html

UFO Sightings in Canada, www.ufoinfo.com/sightings/canada.shtml

Extraterrestrial Contact, Scientific Study of the UFO Phenomenon
    and the Search for Extraterrestrial Life, www.ufoevidence.
    org/topics/canada.htm

Crop Circles

http://davidpratt.info/cropcirc2.htm

http://paranormal.about.com/od/cropcircles/a/Crop-Circles-
    Best-Evidence.htm

www.bibliotecapleyades.net/circulos_cultivos/esp_
    circuloscultivos14.htm

www.cropcircleresearch.com/

www.cropcirclesecrets.org/education.html

www.manchester.com/features/crop.php

Supporting Sites

St. Paul's UFO Landing Site, ww.stpaulchamber.ca/ufolanding.html

Thomas Reuters Foundation (on radiation levels), www.trust.
org/alertnet/news/factbox-how-much-radiation-is-dangerous/

L'Anse aux Meadows, http://whc.unesco.org/en/list/4

www.thecanadianencyclopedia.com/index.cfm?PgNm=TCE&Pa
rams=A1ARTA0004527

Tracerlab and other equipment, www.orau.org/ptp/collection/
surveymeters/tracerlabsu14.htm

PRWeb, www.prweb.com/releases/2009/03/prweb2264574.htm

Shag Harbour Museum, http://cuun.i2ce.com/misc/
shagHarbourMuseum/

Alien Abductions

www.ufobc.ca/experience/version

www.ufobc.ca/yukon/n-canol-abd/index.htm

About the Author

Lisa Wojna

Lisa is the author of six other non-fiction books for Folklore Publishing, and without a doubt, anything mysterious is apt to catch her attention. Her research has taken her down trails she never would have expected, and she has discovered a great deal that is strange and weird about our great country. Lisa has worked in the community newspaper industry as a writer and journalist and has travelled all over Canada from the windy prairies of Manitoba to northern British Columbia and even to the wilds of Africa. Writing and photography have always been a central part of her life, but it's the people behind every story that keep her motivated and excited.